Our

Dear

Child

Our

Dear

Child

Letters to your baby on the way

DENISE & TIMOTHY GEORGE

CHRISTIAN FOCUS

© 2006 Denise & Timothy George

ISBN 1-84550-141-1
ISBN 978-1-84550-141-9

10 9 8 7 6 5 4 3 2 1

Published in 2006
by
Christian Focus Publications, Ltd.
Geanies House, Fearn, Tain,
Ross-shire, IV20 1TW, Great Britain.

www.christianfocus.com

Cover Design by Moose77.com

Printed and bound by
Bercker, Germany

Dedication:
For
Christian Timothy George,
our firstborn

Introduction

One early September morning, our first child was born. We had waited a long time for our baby. We discovered, during the nine more months we waited for him, that pregnancy is not only a physical event for the mom, but also an emotional and spiritual event for both the mom and dad. We shared many golden moments during those long months of pregnancy, as we anticipated his birth.

From the early days of pregnancy, we decided to record our thoughts as a future mother and father – our hopes, prayers and dreams – so that one day our child, a son as he turned out to be, would know the events which led up to his birth. We wrote many personal letters to our unborn baby, and, on occasion, we shared them with close friends.

We had no plans to make them public/ to share them with a wider audience until a friend suggested that we consider publication.

"I know it will be hard to expose and share your most tender, private thoughts," he told us, "but don't you think the world needs a little tenderness?" That's how *Our Dear Child* came to be.

Later, we journeyed again into pregnancy and expectation when we waited with great anticipation for the arrival of our unborn daughter. That experience delivered the same excitement, golden moments, hopes, prayers and dreams. Each child – unique, special, individual, a gift from God – a miracle.

We pray that you will enjoy these letters, whether you are expecting a child or grandchild, rejoicing in the anticipated birth of a friend's baby, or just unabashedly in love with babies in general.

Denise and Timothy George
Birmingham, Alabama, 2006

Prelude

Letters to an Unborn Child

Dear Child,

Up in the attic, tied with pale blue ribbons, are 400 letters written to us by our loving Grandmother Williams. She wrote more than one letter a week for over seven years while we were students in Cambridge, Massachusetts.

Through these "love notes", my grandmother reminded us that we were still a very important part of the family even though we lived a thousand miles away. These letters will always be precious to us, as they communicate a part of our family history that, unless recorded, would be lost from memory over the years.

Why do we write these letters to you, our unborn child? Because through these "love notes" you will learn of the days before your birth. These are a part of your family history, our family history, details that will, no doubt, fade from our thoughts over the years.

As you read these pages one day in the future, you will know of our hoping, our waiting, and our planning for you before you "officially" entered our world. You will learn of the many things we hold dear: our faith, our family, our beliefs, our values.

And, little one, we pray that one day, perhaps in your own attic, you will hold within pale blue ribbons these letters, a recorded reminder of our love for you – a very important part of our family.

Love, Mom and Dad

1: Discovery – We're Going to Have a Baby!

* * * * *

"Thou didst knit me together in my mother's womb."
(Ps. 139:13)

Are You for Real?

Dear Child,

No experience in life can equal the joy and delight of discovering you will be the mother of a baby! We wondered. We waited. We felt great excitement at the prospect of a pregnancy, but we wouldn't let ourselves get too excited, just in case the pregnancy wasn't real.

When our doctor announced the results of the pregnancy test – yes, the test was positive! – we felt elated. I must admit, I haven't thought about much else since, nor am I likely to until you are born. I scan every store catalog for the latest in baby clothes. I notice every baby in every shop, in every car, and everywhere I go. I comb through bookstores, buying up books that will give me some much-needed guidance on pregnancy, childbirth and child rearing.

I can hardly wait to hold you in my arms, to cuddle, to soothe, to rock you to sleep at night. I want to dress you in tiny clothes, snuggle you in soft blankets, and show you off to my family and friends.

I feel deep responsibility, too, for your upbringing. I have thought deeply about your physical health and needs, your mental and educational requirements, and your emotional and spiritual development. I know your dad and I are responsible for your new life – you, who will depend on us for your very existence – and that will be a great responsibility. But we are excited, eager and ready to get started.

Are you for real? Yes, child. You are very real!

Love, Mom

The Miracle of Life

Dear Child,

How often we hear the phrase the "miracle of life". In the rightly given context of a sentence, it rolls naturally off our tongues like other automatic sayings which have long lost their freshness and meaning. The "miracle of life" was but another tired cliché until the miracle happened to us!

Your mother and I marvel at the wonder of conception. It begins with a desire for a child, a sperm, an egg, exact timing, a period of incubation, and ends with a human life – five tiny fingers on each hand and five tiny toes on each foot – priceless, unique in its existence. How could this be?!

Your mother and I read the prenatal books in disbelief: nine weeks after conception, your face is completely formed. At three months, you have fingernails and can make tiny fists. At four months, you have eyebrows, eyelashes, and you can suck your thumb. At six months, your eyes are open and you can hear sound! Amazing! Scientists can partially explain this phenomenon, but perhaps even their highly trained minds cannot comprehend it fully.

But prenatal development – the making of a baby – is more than biological. It is a mother and father waiting in anticipation, hoping, praying, and preparing for the infant's entry into the world. It is loving the child in the early stages, even before he is fully formed. It is planning for the baby's future. It is a mysterious process which joins us with the Creator himself.

Surely, life is a miracle!

Love, Dad

Before You Were You

Dear Child,

I have been thinking a lot lately about where you came from. Yes, of course, I know about as much as someone who is not a medical specialist can concerning what school children sometimes call "the birds and the bees". You as a unique, particular person, with a set of chromosomes and genes never put together before in just this pattern, came into being inside the body of your mother through the normal process of human procreation. You did not pre-exist in some other life, nor will you be reincarnated as some other form of being in the future. You are you.

But before you were you, you did exist in the mind of God. Your heavenly Father foreknew you from all eternity. The psalmist David said to the Lord, "All the days ordained for me were written in your Book before one of them came to be" (Ps. 139:16). To the prophet Jeremiah, God said, "Before I formed you in the womb I knew you, before you were born I set you apart; I appointed you as a prophet to the nations" (Jer. 1:5).

When the Bible says that God "knew" you before you were born, that means that God has a special plan and purpose for your life. You are not an accident thrown at random into the universe; nor are you a pre-packaged clump of cells whose destiny is controlled in some fatalistic way by the pull of gravity or the course of the stars. No, you are a "person", made in the image of God, intended from all eternity to come into being at this precise moment of history.

There are many things about your future I do not know. What will be the exact date of your birth? Will blue or green be your favorite color? When will you get married, and to whom? Will you have many – or any – children of your own? What will you do with your life? The future, your future, stretches out before us now as a great unknown. But God knows all of these things, and everything else. He is never caught off guard by anything that happens, to us or to anyone else.

Some people think that to believe in such a God is to stifle human creativity and freedom. I don't agree. It means instead that you can move with joy, confidence and purpose, knowing that the steps of your life are ordered by a great and gracious heavenly Father, and the one who has already been to the future and has come back to say to us, "Be not afraid!"

Love, Dad

Sharing the News

Dear Child,

So far one of the most exciting aspects of your future birth has been sharing the news of the pregnancy. Listen as we eavesdrop on some of the announcements.

"Hello, Mom and Dad," I greeted your maternal grandparents-to-be by long-distance telephone. "How do you feel about becoming grandparents?" I asked. Considering that your grandparents, especially your grandmother, has been a patient soul and has waited some eleven years to hear such news, it was understandable that, at first, she did not believe the good news.

"Oh," she asked calmly. "Are you going to adopt?"

"No Mom," I answered. "We're going to give birth!"

To which she questioned repeatedly: "Are you sure?! Are you sure?!"

Only after I had convinced her that the discovery was, indeed, based on fact, did she join in on the excitement.

For the next thirty minutes or so, long after your grandfather had hung up the telephone extension (because he couldn't get even one word in), Mom and I planned everything, from when you should start on cereal to what color your clothes should be.

Next, we phoned long-distance your maternal great-grandparents-to-be. Endowed with more faith in immediately believing good news from their granddaughter, their enthusiasm and squeals of joy began before I even finished the "how do you feel about becoming great-grandparents again?" After a few minutes of rejoicing, my grandmother confessed, "Denise, we thought it would never happen." We spent the next few hours calling more family members and friends all over the country. To those around the world whom we could not afford to call, we wrote letters. Their reactions were somewhat the same: very pleased that we were to know the great love and happiness brought by the birth of a child.

Like a tiny pebble tossed into a pool of water, the news of your early existence has spread among all those whom we hold dear. The ripples have drifted out to include our circle of family and friends in the realm of joy that we have already felt. Birth, little one, is indeed a family affair. And the love and concern of many for you now will be magnified a hundredfold when you are born, making your new world a warmly inviting place to be.

Love, Mom

2. Reflections – To Be a Parent

*****

"O Lord of Hosts,…if thou wilt not forget me but grant me offspring, then I will give the child to the Lord for his whole life." (1 Sam. 1:11 NEB)

Thoughts on Motherhood

Dear Child,

The house is still and quiet. You and I are alone. On this warm afternoon, I sit in the porch swing and rock you gently. Back and forth. Back and forth. I hope you are comforted by the gentle rocking motion. You seem content. You seem happy. Only the sounds of chirping birds and the occasional bark of a neighborhood dog break the treasured silence. Time has ceased to be. We, alone and together, share the beauty of this moment; a memorable, precious moment; a time to reflect, to dream. I wait for you in the outside world. You wait to be born from the inside world. Amazing, this mysterious way God has designed pregnancy and birth.

My mind wanders only once to the work that awaits me: the wet clothes in the washer, the dishes in the sink, the overdue bills on my desk. How unimportant those mundane chores seem, compared to this precious time spent with you – mother and unborn child! The clothes, dishes and bills will always be before me. But our time together – mother and unborn child – will pass by quickly.

I continue to rock, realizing that by tomorrow, this afternoon will be only a brief memory to be filed with a succession of other memories. I place my hand on my left side and feel your light, quick movement. Do you somehow know the excitement and pleasure you have brought me? How I anticipate the day of your arrival, when I can cuddle you in my arms and gaze upon your delicate, fully formed features!

I will soon become a mother. No, I am a mother already. What difference does a few months make, whether I hold you in my womb or hold you in my arms? You are my child. Either way, I hold you close to me, under my heart. Your presence has changed my very existence.

Even now I care for you. I choose the food which nourishes you. I would protect you from harm with my life. I am concerned about your safety and health. I think about you always. I consider your future in every decision I make. The responsibility for your life, even now, weighs heavily on me.

The house is still and quiet. For a few precious moments, you and I are alone. Time has ceased to be. Together, we share the beauty of this fast-fleeting moment. As we journey through life together, my lovely child, may we have many more moments like these: memorable moments, precious moments … mother and child moments.

Love, Mom

Will I Love You?

Dear Child,

Will I love you? I cringe at the very thought of such an honest question. My grandmother – so dedicated to her children, grandchildren and great-grandchildren – would be shocked if she could read my unspoken thoughts. Of course you will love your child, she would probably quickly tell me. But surely the thought must, at least once or twice, cross the mind of the average mother-to-be?

Yes, I do long for your birth. I look forward to a normal waistline again. I anticipate a cup of steaming, caffeine-laden coffee with cream and sugar, without feeling guilt pangs over your fetal health. I can hardly wait to see you. Will you inherit your father's blue eyes and blonde hair, or my dark eyes and dark hair? Will you be a boy or a girl? I have many unanswered questions, little one, you who are so near to my heart, yet so far from my vision.

You are my mystery, kept hidden from me for a short time, soon to be revealed, and all my ponderings answered. Yes, little one, I do anxiously yearn for your birth, but the "love" question rings in my heart again and again. Sometimes I hear the question faintly. Sometimes the question comes at such a loud volume that it blocks out all my other concerns.

Will I love, child – you, whom I have never met, yet whom I know so intimately well? Our heart beats mesh, we breathe and take nourishment as one, yet I feel no strong, overwhelming maternal "love" instinct within me. Not yet, anyway.

"Wait until you see his little round face and hold him in your arms, then you'll feel 'motherly' toward him," a friend tells me. "But," I ask her, "what if that doesn't happen?" She has no answer.

I once saw a film about a magical love potion someone poured into the New York City water system. Everyone who drank it immediately felt brotherly love toward one another. The potion had an instant and dramatic effect on all who sipped it. Will that be the case here, little one? Will I see your face and feel deepest love for you? Or will love come from caring for you daily? Will love come at all?

My friend tells me I worry about something that will never be. "All mothers love their babies," she tells me.

But do not all mothers-to-be sometimes worry about whether or not they will love their babies? I'm sure most dare not voice their concern. I am being quite open and honest with you, dear child. At times I feel I love you more than anything or anyone in the entire world. At other times, however, the emotion of love barely fills me.

Will I love you? I do not know. What is love, anyway? Is love:
- an expectant mother watching every bite she puts into her mouth lest she hurt her unborn child's health?
- or getting the required number of resting and sleeping hours?
- or being faithful to regular doctor's appointments?
- or protecting her fetus with all her might?
- or planning for the child's future?
- or praying for the safe delivery of the baby?

If that's the definition of love, little one, I now love you more than life itself! Perhaps love is not so much something a mother feels for her child, but rather all those many things she does for her child – those day-to-day clothes changes, those long sleepless nights, and those efforts to soothe a fussy cry. Perhaps "feelings of love" have very little to do with actual love. Surely love is a verb, and not a noun!

Will I love you? Indeed! I already do!

Love, Mom

To work or Not to work

Dear Child,

I have a big decision to make soon. After your birth, should I work outside the home or should I work solely inside the home? Or can I somehow figure out how to do both? Should I postpone my career and devote all my time to you and our home? Or should I continue my busy career schedule and seek some capable childcare help for you? A preschool program perhaps?

I am pulled between two strong forces. On the one hand, I'd love nothing better than to cuddle you and care for you every minute of every day. But on the other hand, I have a desire to continue to reach out and help others – my outside employment – and that takes great time and energy.

Unlike many other working moms, who must work outside the home as a financial necessity, at this point in our lives I can choose to work outside the home or not. Granted, we can't afford any frills, and our savings account hit zero years ago. Surely, the decision would be an easier one if I had no choice in the matter.

In many ways, I'd enjoy the role of full-time mother. While homemaking, cooking and caring for a family are certainly demanding work, combining a career with the house and family responsibilities would prove much more difficult. I just don't know if I could physically do it all.

I wonder if all mothers-to-be struggle with the decision to quit outside jobs and work solely inside the home? It's a choice that men in our society seldom have to face.

I pray, little one, that our loving Father will give me the strength and ability to give my best to him and, at the same time, to give my best to you. May he guide me in this decision and all the other significant decisions I will be called to make on account of approaching motherhood. Surely, little one, I will make all these decisions through prayer, and always with you first in my mind and heart.

Love, Mom

Daddyhood

Dear Child,

What is it going to feel like to be a daddy? I know I will be proud, happy, exhilarated, but probably also a little afraid, unsure, awkward. I hope you will help me learn the ropes of fatherhood.

I want to tell you a little bit about my father. I never knew him very well. He suffered from a disease called alcoholism and died when I was only twelve. When he was drinking, he could be very mean, selfish, and impossible to live with.

But there was another side to him as well: a loving, gentle, caring side. I remember walking all the way to town with him one day. He spent the last nickel he had to buy me a grape Nehi. When he was sober, he took us to church, taught us to read, made sure we had a new pair of shoes every winter. I have long forgiven him for the times he made us unhappy. I am only sorry that I never got to know him better.

Somehow, growing up without a full-time father has made me all the more anxious to be a daddy myself. I want to give you all the things I never had. I want to love you and hug you the way I wish my father had loved and hugged me. I want to play ping-pong and tennis with you, teach you to love Shakespeare and Bach, show you Monticello and the Grand Canyon. You see, I have your childhood already mapped out! Deep down I know that I will have to let you be you – not an extension of me. Relationship is what being a father is all about, and relationship implies risk. I am willing to take the risk if you are.

Of all the words that Jesus used to describe God, his favorite word was Abba. It's a word which comes from the language of babies, made from the kinds of sounds that you will soon be uttering: ba-ba, da-da, ab-ba. It means just daddy, papa. And this is how Jesus taught us to address our Heavenly Father: Our Abba who art in heaven, hallowed be thy name. If God has chosen this relationship to picture his love for us, then it must be a very special relationship indeed.

Love, Dad

An Experience Missed?

Dear Child,

Is your daddy missing the child-bearing experience – a happening both pleasurable and disagreeable? I feel both bliss and blue that only I should be allowed to carry you and to bear you.

Mary considered herself "blessed" to have carried the Lord Jesus. I have felt blessed, too, little one, since the first day I discovered you were on the way. Your father has felt the excitement too, but can he feel the same excitement as I?

Fortunately your dad has been spared the discomforts of pregnancy: the first few months of morning sickness, the bloated and out of proportion body, the tired legs and swollen feet. But he has also missed your first movement, the little kick in the side that resembled an abdomen full of tiny minnows splashing happily in a watery home. What mother-to-be can feel the life within her stir and not be forever moved? Your dad has felt pride in having fathered you, but no pride can compare with the satisfaction of nourishing and carrying a developing child within a body full term: a life within a life.

For the delivery, your father will be right there, standing by our side, waiting, praying, anticipating along with us. But can the glory of your birth, your being released from my body, be experienced as profoundly by him as by me?

No doubt this experience will be exhilarating for both me and your dad, but how wonderful it would be if nature allowed both the mother and the father to physically experience child-bearing and childbirth! Why must a woman alone be given the depth of blessedness, while the man stands at the sidelines, a second party to the advent, participating, yet not fully experiencing?

But, little one, perhaps your father has not missed the experience after all. The beauty of participation may dwell not so much in the state of motherhood or fatherhood as in parenthood – a mutual blessedness, that greatest of all happenings that a husband and wife can experience jointly.

Love, Mom

It shouldn't Hurt to Be a child

Dear Child,

It shouldn't hurt to be a child. Yet all over the world, children are physically and verbally abused and neglected every day.

Not long ago, we read the story of a young mother who scalded her seven-month-old baby boy to death. "I went to the stove, heated the water, put my son in the kitchen sink, then poured the boiling water over his head and body," she told the authorities. She continued her startling account: "Then I heated more water and poured it on my baby."

I wonder what crossed that child's mind, as his most trusted companion spilled boiling water down his small, writhing body? What terrible agony that little boy endured at the hands of his own mother! "Can't you hear that baby's screams?" a lawyer asked the jury during the mother's trial.

I heard recently about a mother who had calmly cut off her baby daughter's arms. Then she called the police and told them what she had done! Her daughter died not long after the police arrived. What crossed that little girl's mind, when her own mother took a knife and butchered her young body, cutting off her arms?

We read articles and hear news reports like this with a hurting heart and tears in our eyes. Imagine, a young child – so vulnerable, so naturally loving, so completely helpless, a baby who looks to his mother as number one protector and caretaker from the dangers of the world – being tortured by the one who helped give him life.

Can't we hear the cries of thousands of defenseless children who bear the marks and scars of parental abuse? Rapes, beatings, whippings, drownings, severe mistreatment, harsh words, debilitating name calling, neglect: we wonder how parents can treat the most precious of all people – children – in this way. We live in a society that must be reminded often to pay attention to our children. A popular slogan asks: "Have you hugged your kids today?" Do we really get so caught up in our work and the mundane activities of everyday life that we forget to show attention to our little people?

As a nation, we do sometimes neglect our children. We once heard a commentator in a documentary on children in the United States state that our children have no place in our society. Our culture is oriented to adults, not to children. Most of our restaurants, shopping centers and parks have no special facilities for youngsters. He ended the program with this thought-grabbing statement: "If a visitor arrived from outer space, would he know that children even lived here?"

Jesus loved children. His actions proved that. He once told his disciples to let the little children come to him. He gathered them on his lap and made them an example for all adults to see and to strive for.

Yet many adults, mothers and fathers of the world, ignore Jesus' words and actions. How many innocent beings must suffer at the hands of their parents: the hitting, kicking, shaking, confining? One caseworker reported a father using his young son for firewood; another reported that a mother shook her infant until he died.

Such parental bullying goes undetected in most cases, as babies can't talk to tell of their day-to-day suffering. They must wait patiently and painfully until someone discovers the unevenly mended bone, the scar tissue or cigarette burn. Many of these little ones are killed or maimed, and many more scarred for life, having to endure a childhood of abuse, afraid of the pain each day may bring, never knowing kind words and affectionate attention and strong, loving arms. Surely, it shouldn't hurt to be a child!

Our Dear Child ✱ ✱ ✱ ✱ ✱

Little one, you can be assured that we will do all in our power to ensure you a happy and joyous childhood. You will never have to fear the adults around you, as we will not lift a hand to you in anger. You will be treated with love, patience, respect and understanding, spoken to kindly and softly, and will be considered an important and precious part of our family.

Love, Mom and Dad

If You Are a
Special-Needs Child

Dear Child,

I am frequently asked these days: "Do you want a girl or a boy?"

"It doesn't matter," I respond, and then add, "as long as the baby is healthy."

"As long as the baby is healthy…" The words ring in my ears long after I've said them.

From conception till birth every parent hopes for a healthy, perfect baby. Upon delivery, anxious mothers and fathers count toes and fingers and check every inch for newborn perfection.

Now, able to peek into the privacy of the womb, medical scientists can direct expectant parents to make fetal life and death decisions based on their unborn child's health. Hence, moral, ethical and social questions abound. Should special-needs babies be allowed or denied birth? Are human beings capable of making such decisions? Do special-needs people have a place in our populace, or are they simply a strain on the taxpayer's dollar, a burden on the shoulders of society?

Theological questions are raised. Why does God allow the less than perfect development of a child? Could he not spare these innocent infants a life of disease and pain if he wanted to? What about the parents? How should they view their deformed newborn? As a special gift from God, who entrusts this baby only to those parents he thinks capable, or as an embarrassment – the sins of their fathers passed through the generations?

The questions are too numerous, the answers unobtainable.

Little child, when you are born, you may not have a perfect body. You may not be able to see or hear or walk. If so, will your father and I be able to deal with your limitations? Are we strong enough to cope? Emotionally? Spiritually? I wonder. Will the rest of the family become silent, unable to find consoling words for our misfortune? Will they pity us and you? I couldn't bear that. I may blame myself for your deformity, since you were placed in my womb for your fetal care. Did I eat the right foods, or get enough rest? As the time of your birth approaches, my fears heighten. How I want you to be so perfect – the most beautiful baby in the hospital's Plexiglas cubicle!

Then I stop. I look around me and make a startling discovery. I see no perfect human beings! A hot temper, a selfish attitude, an unsympathetic heart – we are all less than perfect in many ways. With alcohol dependence, drug addiction and bodily abuse, we destroy ourselves. Through war, hatred and greed, we destroy each other.

Who then has the right to cast away or even pity the child with a missing arm or open spine? Whom should we pity more: the whole one who has no love for God, himself or others, who takes for granted a healthy, pain-free body; or the physically imperfect one who gives thanks for the faculties he does possess and who, through a lifetime of long and hard struggle, has found peace with God, himself and others?

I look at my friends. After the first appearance or two, I fail to notice the physical deficiencies of those I have come to know and love.

My friend, Helen, cannot see. She has been sightless since birth. Yet few people have lived a fuller life. A professional writer and author, a gifted speaker, an active church worker, Helen has found happiness and success without eyes. Helen "sees" another person from the inside out, judging beauty by a kind act, an understanding voice, and a loving attitude. She does not form her opinions of a person by the color of one's skin, the shape of one's nose, or the condition of one's clothes. How much more blind is the person who is limited by prejudices!

Another friend, Ginger, cannot walk. Strapped to a wheelchair, her small frame is deformed and twisted, her bones so brittle they often break with a sudden sneeze. Yet Ginger is a cheerful and ambitious young woman, always smiling, a delight and encouragement to her friends. A sophomore in college, she works hard and makes good grades. She has even learned to drive a specially-equipped car. Ginger's world is joyful even though racked with constant pain. How much more limited is the person who wallows in self-pity, who lacks ambition and hope, and who lives in defeat and despair, than the one whose only limitation is an unco-operative body!

So, my little child, God has already formed you. He has already shaped your tiny body. Soon, you'll be ready for delivery into the world. Be it perfect or imperfect, healthy or diseased, strong or weak, you must wear your body with thanksgiving and pride.

And remember this always: only part of you is physical. You have a body, yes, but you also have a mind, whose vastness has yet to be measured – and you have a spirit. The spirit runs free, if you will let it, and knows no limitation.

Love, Mom

Our Prayers and Our Promises

Dear Child,

As your parents-to-be, as the partners who will care for you from infancy to adulthood, let us share with you our prayers and our promises.

We pray that we might be good caretakers, kind and loving parents, having the wisdom to teach you, to counsel you, and to always be there whenever you need us.

We pray that through our joint efforts we can create a happy home for you. May you have a fanciful and fun-filled childhood, free from danger and fear – a childhood that you will keep in your heart and memory long after you've left us for a life of your own.

We pray that we can provide for you a proper education, the acquisition of knowledge that will begin the moment you open your eyes and look at your new environment, one that will continue throughout a lifetime. Your future will be your decision, but we will strive through education to build a solid base, one that will bring dreams and ambitions within your reach.

We pray that we will love and treat with kindness the spouse you may one day choose, if you decide to marry, and the children born into your home. We will consider them as part of our family and will open our home to them as their home, a booth in the wilderness, where they too can find rest, comfort and sincere affection.

Those are our prayers for you.

Our promises to you, little one, are these:

We promise to care for you after birth just as we do now before birth, in the best way we can. May we be close by to bandage your scratches, to safeguard your tender feelings, and to keep watch on those feverish nights when you are ill.

We promise to always love you. Our strong circle of love will enclose you, whether or not we agree with you, whether or not you even want our love.

We promise to protect you, to keep you well nourished, to provide a warm shelter, and to shield you as much as possible from grief and worry.

We promise our eternal devotion to you, regardless of mental, emotional, or physical handicaps you may have at birth or may be afflicted with during your lifetime. Our dedication to you will not be compromised by what society terms "human flaws". You will be given the right to life, a life only God himself can give or take away.

We promise to respect you as a person with rights and opinions. We will value your ideas and judgments, no matter how immature your years. You will have a rightful place in this family – that of a respected and beloved member.

We promise to be kind to you both in speech and actions. We will approach you only with soft and considerate words. May our actions always prove our love for you.

We promise to give you guidelines and to discipline you. We will strive to make you a responsible child, a person you will like, one who will be accepted and admired by others. We will punish you only when necessary. Our "no's" will be accompanied with good reason and explanation. Punishment will not be directed toward you in anger or un-thoughtfulness. Discipline will be firm, but will never evoke pain or the slightest physical or emotional discomfort of any kind.

We promise to teach you to respect other people and their property, to put yourself in their shoes in your day-to-day dealings with them, to regard them as we regard you – an individual with rights and feelings. We will teach you to respect all of God's creatures and to realize that they too experience affection when loved and pain when hurt.

We will teach you to respect nature, the cycle of life which, once destroyed, cannot be re-created; the tree cut down will stay the tree cut down.

We promise to help you learn the value of money. Let us teach you to "share the wealth", to use your money for the upgrading and uplifting of others, to regard it as something you control but which does not control you, to put it in proper perspective in light of far more important things.

We promise to nurture you spiritually, to teach you of God and his love made flesh through his Son. Family devotions, church worship, prayers before meals – you will know of all these things.

And, finally, we promise to teach you the value of a worthwhile life, not by society's standards but by God's standards. As will be dramatically illustrated by your birth, your life is a gift to us. May you also consider it a gift, each moment of it, and live life to its fullest, always with cleanliness, honesty, integrity and honor, forever being thankful to God for the gift of your existence.

These are our prayers for you and our promises to you, little child. May God help us to uphold them in our hearts and to practice them in our home.

Love, Dad

3. Anticipation - Let's Get Ready!

* * * * *

"Prepare your minds for action." (1 Peter 1:13)

The "New Baby" List

Dear Child,

Shirts, gowns, and overalls,
The baby's list I heed,
Sweaters, hats, clothing bag,
All these things you'll need!
Stroller, rattles, baby scale,
The books state what I seek,
Lotion, powder and cleansing gel,
And eighty bottles a week!
Dishes, spoons, forks and bib,
For eating sets the mood,
Cabinets full of cups and caps,
But can I find the food?!
Towels, cloths, baby soap,
"The bathroom's full!" I laugh.
Shampoo, sponge, brush and comb,
Why, we'll never take a bath!
Blanket, bed, bumper guard,
A mattress firm is best,
With sheets, pad, Teddy bears,
I hope you can find rest!
Chest of drawers and auto seat,
"Our budget's blown!" Dad speaks.
But, I inform him with great dread,
"That's just for the first six weeks!"

curious George

Dear Child,

The baby gifts have already started to come. How exciting to open the ribbons and bows and boxes, and to discover the love of family and friends! Surely, the one favorite gift so far has been a brown, furry monkey with a red nose, bulging eyes, and soft, cuddly stuffing. His name? "Curious George." "Curious" came from a friend and colleague who thought a monkey named "Curious" and "George" would be appropriate.

A note came attached to Curious' jacket. "Curious is an appropriate gift for you," the giver wrote, "since any child of yours is bound to be curious about all kinds of things – himself, the world, and the mystery we call God."

I hope he was right about your being curious. Theologians used to rail against what they called "vain curiosity". A far greater vice, I think, is the squelching of curiosity. Curious Columbus sailed into the unknown and stumbled onto a continent. Curious Einstein refused to quit thinking and uncovered the secrets of the atom.

Who knows what you and Curious George might discover? Human babies, unlike some other species, are born with their eyes open. I hope that your eyes and mind will always stay open to the wonder, surprise and ever-unfolding mystery which await you on this side of birth.

Love, Dad

choosing Your Name

Dear Child,

Well, we have finally agreed. The perennial problem of name-bestowing has beset your mother and me since first we learned that you were on the way. How to decide - should your mother choose one name and I choose the other? Not fair, she said, since George would be your last name anyway, and that would give me two names to her one. For a while we said that if you were a girl, she would do the naming, and if you were a boy, then I would make the choice.

That was fine until I announced my projected nomenclature: Calvin Augustinus George. Then we were back to scratch. If you are a boy, the fight will probably go on till birthing time, but if you are a girl, we have had a meeting of minds – your name will be Alyce Elizabeth George.

The Alyce is for Alice Crane Williams, your great-grandmother on your mother's side, "Mama" to all of us younger ones in the family and "Trick" to Papa since first he carried her – the prettiest thing he had ever seen, he said – on the handlebars of his bicycle on Sand Mountain long ago. For sixty-two years she has been the wife of George M. Williams, barber, preacher, itinerant evangelist and singer. She put up peach preserves on the day of her wedding in 1919 before ever Bud or Ginya or Eenie had been born.

Small, sick, weakly, given up by doctors long ago, but tougher than those grim prognosticators knew, she has lived to see a man walk on the moon. Soon you will be the seventh great-grandchild she will have nestled close against her breast.

She loved your mum, and cuddled her when she was small. She carried her on her hip, fed her cabbage from the stove, and told her tales of Granny Crane and long-lost memories of the great War Between the States (United States).

Mama never makes waves, but her quiet strength and gentle love have left their mark on your mother and on nameless others who have felt her touch. I wish for you her timeworn faith, her loyalty and love which know no stint, and above all her enormous power to care for those who hurt, as she herself has hurt so long and so bravely. So bear the name of your great-grandmother with pride, for it is hewn from precious stone.

Elizabeth is for Mary Elizabeth George, your great-great-aunt on my father's side, with whom I lived from ages one to six, and again from twelve to seventeen. Apart from dipping Bruton's snuff, she had no habits good or bad that I knew of. Widowed early on in life, she retained a matronly beauty, enough so that Old Man Smith wanted to marry her when she was well into her sixties. But she said, "No thanks!"

She was reared in Tennessee, in a Republican pocket which never seceded from the Union during the United States' Civil War. She remembered when William Jennings Bryan ran for president against William McKinley, and the zealots sang at a political rally: "We'll hang Billy Bryan from a sour apple tree." She never did vote herself though, for she could hardly trace the letters which spelled her name.

I remember her walking me to the first grade every day, taking up for me when Billy Nash bloodied my nose, and going with me every Sunday to the country-church-in-the-city near our rented house. Pastor Linkous would pat my head and call me his little preacher boy, and Aunt Mary smiled and said it was a nice thing for him to say. And years later, when she was staying with your mum and me during an illness, I overheard her pray for us one night: that we would always be happy, have each other near, and always trust the Lord to be our strength.

I think she would be proud to know that since then our love has weathered eleven years. I think she would be very proud to hold you in her arms and sing to you of Jesus' love as once she sang to me. Wear Elizabeth well, for it bespeaks an unknown saint whose grace may dwell in you.

Alice Crane Williams, Mary Elizabeth George – Mama and Aunt Mary: simple women – two lives which hardly rippled the surface of their times, but these lives were so filled with love they touched us in the depths. They are a part of us, and they are also a part of you, and so we pass along their goodly names.

Love, Dad

Bible Stories

Dear Child,

As soon as you get home from the hospital, and are able to be held in my arms, I plan to begin reading to you, one chapter per night, from the Holy Scriptures. I think we'll begin with the Psalms. Somehow I believe that just reading the Bible to you out loud will have some long-lasting effect on your spiritual life and formation in Christ in the future. "The Word of God is alive and powerful," the Bible says (Heb. 4:12).

As you grow older, I hope you will come to know and love the Bible in a personal way. The Bible is far more than merely a book of interesting stories from the ancient world. The Bible is the very word of God – inspired by the Holy Spirit and free from all error in everything it says and teaches. Jesus Christ is the living Word of God and the Bible is his written word.

There may come a time, later in your life, when you are tempted to doubt the truthfulness of the Bible. Always remember: God's Word will still be around when all of the scoffers and mockers have fallen into the dust. The Bible's history is historical and the Bible's miracles are miraculous. What the Bible says, God says. What the Bible says happened, really happened. You can count on this for all time and eternity.

But I want you to know more than just a doctrine about the Bible, however important that may be. The Bible will be your spiritual nourishment. "When your words came, I ate them; they were my joy and my heart's delight, for I bear your name, O LORD God Almighty." said the prophet Jeremiah (Jer. 15:16). "Your word is a lamp to my feet and a light for my path," said the psalmist (Ps. 119:105).

We do not worship the Bible, but we worship the God of the Bible, the God who has revealed Himself to us in His Son, Jesus Christ. I hope to teach you to memorize the Scriptures, to honor and love the Word of God, which will sustain you in times of temptation and testing, and which will bring you comfort as you walk through the valley of the shadow of death.

Among the very last words the Apostle Paul wrote from his prison cell in Rome was this request, addressed to his son in the faith, Timothy: "Do your best to come to me quickly...when you come, bring the cloak that I left with Carpus at Troaz, and my scrolls, especially the parchments" (2 Tim. 4:9, 13). The scrolls he referred to must surely have been the Holy Scriptures, in his case the Old Testament, perhaps the very Psalms I shall soon be reading to you. When you come to the end of your own life, may the words of the Bible still echo in your heart: "The Lord is my shepherd, I shall not want...to You, oh Lord, I lift up my soul; in You I trust, oh my God...the Lord is my light and my salvation – whom shall I fear...for the Lord is good and His love endures forever; His faithfulness continues through all generations" (Pss. 23:1; 25:1; 27:1; 100:5)

Love, Dad

Your Spiritual Upbringing

Dear Child,

What wonderful preparations your mum and I are making for you! Almost everything is in order and waiting for you, the newest member of our family. Your mother and I have gone to great lengths to plan for your physical, emotional and social needs. Your finished bedroom sits empty in anticipation: new yellow curtains, a designer baby-bed, and a chest of drawers to hold the latest in tot fashions. We've discussed your childcare arrangements, put money aside for your college education, and have attended to every jot and tittle that will concern you.

Your spiritual life has also been a topic of great interest lately, even at this early stage. Your mother and I both have had dedicated spiritual leaders in our lives, working hard to help shape us spiritually. Grandmothers and grandfathers, aunts and friends who took us to church, read the Bible and sang to us. These special people in our lives taught us to love people and to show sympathy for those less fortunate: the sick, the homeless, the children mistreated.

We, too, want to be your spiritual leaders, little one. Your mother and I want to teach you about Jesus. But many questions come to mind as we think about this important task. When should we start? When will you be old enough to understand what we read or tell you? How should we go about your spiritual training? What methods should we use? How will we conduct family worship together so that you will most benefit from it? We've decided not to wait until you are old enough to understand the words we read to you. We will begin your spiritual journey on the day you come home from the hospital. Of course, everything will seem strange to you: the car, the house, the cat (definitely the cat!). But family devotions – the reading of a psalm, the singing of a hymn, and praying together – will seem no less peculiar than all else around you.

Your mum and I remember with fondness all the times our spiritual leaders led us in Bible readings and family devotions. Those were quiet, serious times of thoughtful study, sometimes accompanied with explanations of the Scriptures. Sometimes, even though hardly able to read, we took our turns at Bible reading, stumbling over the "begats" and mispronouncing the big words. But no one ever laughed at those strange literary distortions. Not one of the little cousins made fun of your eight-year-old mum when she changed "though your sins be as…crimson" into "though your sins be as cinnamon"!

Long ago, during those times of family devotions, we, in our own primitive and unique ways, sensed something special had happened. Sitting or kneeling with our loved ones, away from the busy activities of everyday life, we exchanged something very beautiful with each other and with God. We pray that our family devotions with you, little one, will be just as meaningful and precious.

Mealtimes will also be occasions of prayer and thanksgiving for our family. Perhaps a simple, "God is great, God is good" prayer, the Lord's Prayer or an unrehearsed prayer will serve as our table grace. Before breakfast, lunch, snack or supper, our grandparents read from brightly colored cards, each containing one Bible verse, all held in a straight row by a small plastic loaf-of-bread-shaped box. Those Scripture cards are now worn, bent and faded from use, but nonetheless they are still read before the prayer that precedes each meal.

Church worship also holds dear memories for your mother and me. Worship services, dinners on the ground, Vacation Bible Schools – our individual spiritual leaders took us faithfully to worship God with a congregation. We plan to have you dedicated in our church, little one, where we will promise God and our fellow church members to take your spiritual upbringing very seriously.

Our spiritual leaders often used music as a spiritual teaching aid, singing simple songs to us when we were children. These songs taught us of Jesus' love. They sometimes made up their own tunes to fit certain Scripture verses, making singing the songs and learning the Scriptures fun. No doubt, little one, most of your night-time lullabies will be "Jesus Loves the Little Children" and "The B-I-B-L-E."

Christmas, Easter, and other seasonal events will be times of great celebration in our home, each bringing with it certain customs and decorations and songs that you will come to learn and love. Every holiday will be viewed as a time for spiritual emphasis and worship.

Little child, you are already a very special person to us. We have so carefully planned the first few years of your life. Your comfort, your care, your education, your general well-being, are high on our priority list. How much more important are the plans we make for your spiritual education and well-being. Just as our spiritual leaders, through their loving concern for our souls, helped to lay our spiritual groundwork, how we hope to build for you a house set firmly on the rock, a home where the three of us can live, learn, love, and daily commune with God.

Love, Dad

4. Meet the Family

★ ★ ★ ★ ★

"A happy family is but an early heaven."
John Bowring

Your Homemaking Mummy

Dear Child,

I have a confession to make. Your new mummy would not win any awards in the "Mrs. Perfect Homemaker" contest! In fact, the judges probably wouldn't let her even enter the contest! There. I've said it. It didn't hurt as bad as I thought it would.

I do specialize in some areas, but housekeeping is definitely not one of them. While our house has not yet been declared a health hazard, it certainly wouldn't pass the white-glove cleanliness test.

Who cares if cobwebs hang from the light fixtures? No one I know is tall enough to see them. Who goes around the house looking up at the ceiling, anyway? Why not let the spiders be happy? It's their world too.

And, as the cliché goes, no one could eat off my kitchen floor. I scrub it only during semester break – once or twice a year. Anyway, who in the world would WANT to eat off my kitchen floor?! For eating purposes, the kitchen table is much more comfortable.

I don't make the beds every morning. Why should I take all that time? We just unmake them each night. Make them up, unmake them, make them up, unmake them – it seems kind of silly to me.

I usually dust the furniture right before company walks into the room or when the cat starts to sneeze. Whichever comes first.

And I don't do windows anymore! I did wash the windows one summer. I got soaking wet and caught a cold. I climbed out on the second-story window ledge with a bucket of soapy water and a rag, and I did manage to produce a clean window for all my efforts. But that night it rained, and, by morning the window looked like it did before I washed it. At that point I thought: Why should I risk life and limb hanging out a window and taking a cold just to have a clean view? I've not been so foolish since. Some of my friends think I'm an awful housekeeper. They walk into my kitchen, sniff a few times, and then decline my invitations for lunch.

Sometimes when a person is not so hot in the homemaking department, she can prove her worth in the garden. Not so in my case! I once tried to grow green beans. I dug some big holes in the yard, poured in expensive fertilizer, several pounds of store-bought dirt, and one large package of seeds.

I watched. I watered. I waited. The results of my labor? Three green beans. Not even enough for dinner! I figured that with all that hard work and expense for just three green beans, I'd do better to buy them at the grocery store. I've had the same results with flower seeds.

I used to have a neighbor who was the perfect homemaker and gardener. As far as housekeepers and gardeners go, my neighbor was a "10". She hung out her wet laundry on the clothesline by color, size, and shape. She coordinated her trash in matching trash bags. She trimmed her grass with scissors. She dusted the leaves of her house plants, and polished her silver casserole dish after the dinner guests left. She used cloth napkins for her family, bought toilet paper that matched the towels, and cleaned out her perfectly clean basement weekly. She also grew orchids in her attic, waxed her no-wax floors, and ironed the permanent press label in her husband's shirts.

One day I invited her to my house for afternoon tea. She weeded her way through the front yard, fought off our "attack" cat, and took one long look at my coffee-stained teapot. For some reason, after that, she never responded to my invitations.

Next to my "perfect 10" neighbor, I felt like a minus "10". I'll bet she never hid dirty dishes in her oven, or let the cat eat a pork chop off the dining room carpet, or told her husband to choose his clothes for the day out of the clean-clothes basket.

My "perfect" neighbor was also an extraordinary cook and hostess. Her dinner parties were the talk of the town. She actually followed a recipe for her dishes! She served up meals that I couldn't even pronounce. Her dinners were served piping hot, on time, and in crystal containers. She sat at the head of the table in her long formal gown, every hair in place, and her lipstick still fresh. When her guests took a sip of coffee, she quickly and gracefully refilled their cups.

Now my dinner parties are also the talk of the town, but not for the same reason. Most have been outright disasters. I remember three dinners that were particularly catastrophic.

I painfully embarrassed myself at one formal dinner party when I was trying so hard to be graceful. Somehow I missed the chair while sitting down at the table with eight guests. I sat on the floor, stunned, unable to get up, my long evening skirt somewhere around my waist, and my legs pointing to the ceiling like a V.

At another dinner party, one of the guests suddenly became ill after eating my mushroom meatballs, a new recipe I had tried. His wife, a registered nurse, spent the rest of the evening checking his pulse as he lay, lifeless, on our living room sofa. Needless to say, I disposed of the recipe.

I remember one dinner party that, at first glance, seemed destined to go well. Timothy and I cleaned the house, put peppermint candy on the coffee table, and arranged fresh flowers on the dining room table. It was going to be the perfect dinner party – we thought.

The table looked beautiful. Our guests began to arrive one by one, and soon we had eight people walking into the dining room to take their places at the lace-covered table. It was then that I heard a guest gasp. And then another, and another, and still another. I looked straight ahead at the center of the table and could hardly believe my eyes! Balanced between the lighted candles and the fresh flowers was Hegel, our 16-pound cat. He had already finished off the cream in the silver pitcher, had his tail stuck in the cheese dip, and was fast gulping down the tuna casserole. I quickly, and as gracefully as possible, shooed the cat off the table, refilled the cream pitcher, stirred the cheese dip to remove the cat-tail indentation, and added a little more tuna to the tuna casserole. Then I served my guests. For some reason an overwhelming majority of the guests said they weren't very hungry. Later, however, some settled for coffee – without cream.

So much for the perfect dinner party. In our home, they don't exist! As a cook, I can easily identify with the woman who wrote the bestselling cookbook, *Where There's Smoke, There's Supper.*

Little child, how often I've dreamed of being the perfect homemaker – a woman who can bring home the bacon, fry it up in a pan, and never leave a greasy stove. I keep thinking that one of these days I'll become super-organized – the perfect homekeeper. I envision myself like another woman I once knew. Her floor was sparkling clean before she even started to wash it. She looked more dressed up in her floor-waxing dress and heels than I looked in my finest Sunday outfit. She could wax the whole floor – always smiling – and not chip the nail polish on her long, professionally filed nails. And when her well-dressed, scrubbed-faced children came home from school, she met them at the door with a glass of cold milk and homemade double-fudge brownies, not a crumb of which they dropped on her newly waxed floor.

No doubt this woman's husband called her "blessed". But then, my husband also uses the word "blessed" to describe my efforts…this "blessed" house, this "blessed" supper, this "blessed" garden!

Little child, you will soon be born into a home where nothing is especially organized. You won't be able to see your reflection in our dishes. You will never be able to find two socks that match. But, little one, you might just be happier living with a below "10" homemaking mummy. Just think of the advantages: you can get just as dirty as you want and not be constantly popped into the bathtub. You can bring your pet squirrels, turtles and frogs into the living room without maternal complaint. You can use your sleeve to wipe your nose. You'll not have to make up your bed, hang up your clothes, or pick up your toys. And, since I can't cook them, you'll not have to eat fancy foods that you don't like.

Let's face it, little one, you might just find life at the George house filled with fun, freedom, a lot of peanut butter and jelly sandwiches, and a little bit of heaven too!

Love, Mom

Your Pet cat, Hegel

Dear Child,

Ole' Hegel's life's a-changin'
With baby bath and bed,
He sees these things a-coming' in
And is mighty filled with dread.
Ole' Hegel's life's a-changing,
His senses are too keen,
His blue eyes have already changed
To a monster shade of green!

This is a prenatal warning! Prepare yourself to meet Hegel, your pet Siamese cat. You'll "love" him – he's spoiled, jealous, loud, tempestuous, and he throws temper tantrums when he's denied his own way.

A dogcatcher captured Hegel one day; he needed a home, so we took him in. That happened nine years ago, and Hegel has been the "George baby" ever since.

Hegel's bad habits are too numerous to name. He prowls the house at night and keeps us awake, demands a 6:00 a.m. daily breakfast, and fusses at us when we come home too late. Traveling makes him sick, but staying in the kennel while we travel makes him even sicker.

Hegel hasn't been cheap to keep over the years either. The hospital bills for a toe infection cost us a fortune. We've spent even more money for prescription cat food, special ear medicine, vitamin drops and feline flea soap. Hegel especially enjoys the taste of wool – "old moth mouth," we call him. He has devoured portions of your father's woolen sports coat, knitted tie and favorite tennis socks.

Why do we put up with this obstinate creature who has both your mother and father wrapped firmly around his paw? Well, he's a part of our family. He's been with us through thick and thin (mostly thin), good times and bad, through sickness and health....

"Are you going to give Hegel away when the baby comes?" a friend asked us last week.

"Of course not!" we responded in unison. "Anyway," we asked, "who in his right mind would take an elderly cat, eight pounds overweight, in precarious health, who rules the household?"

As you will discover, Siamese cats are snobbish, independent, demanding, quite verbal, and very smart. Hegel senses something's up. He can no longer find your mother's lap to lie on. He knows those tiny lace booties won't fit either your father or me. And the little room upstairs with the new baby bed, dirty-clothes pail, and the "Mary Had a Little Lamb" inscribed on the wall? It has been set up for months and he hasn't seen anyone use it yet! Puzzled, he looks at us as if to ask, "Just what's going on around here, anyway?"

Chances are, Hegel will be jealous of you. He may pack up his litter box and leave. Your father and I have worried about a possible "sibling" rivalry problem. We're reading all the advice the animal experts have to offer.

"Make a tape recording of a screaming baby," they tell us, "and play it over and over to the pet so he'll get used to the noise before the baby comes."

Good idea, I thought. But where do you find a kid who will cry on cue into a tape recorder? And how do you make a baby scream? Pinch it? Withhold its food?

More advice from the experts: "When coming home from the hospital, the new mother and father should walk into the house for the first time without the baby. They should give the animal time alone with them before bringing the infant into the home."

Good idea, I thought. But where does one leave a three-day-old baby while one spends time alone with the pet? In the car? On the back porch?

Well, little one, your father and I have finally come up with a solution of our own. Just how does a couple find peace and tranquility in a home with a spoiled, old cat and a brand new baby? They make house rules, and they post them in plain view:

Rules for Baby:
1. You are not permitted to step on, sit on, or slam the door on the cat's tail.
2. You may not eat the food from Hegel's bowl, nor drink the water from his dish.
3. Playing in the litter box is not allowed.
4. Hegel does not have to share his catnip, his rubber mouse or his tinfoil ball with you.

Rules for Hegel:
1. You are not permitted to bite or nibble the baby's fingers or toes.
2. You may not sleep in the baby's bed, no matter how soft and inviting the new blue blankets are.
3. Swinging in the baby's swing is not allowed.
4. The baby does not have to share his teether, his milk bottle, or his stuffed toys with you.

Here are the rules, little ones! May the best baby win!

Love, Mom

Those Dedicated Workers

Dear Child,

Your new world will be crowded with people who will love and help care for you: family, friends, and church workers.

For all those dedicated workers –

who will comfort you when you cry;

who will keep your clothes and blankets dry;

who will help feed and nourish you;

who will help you explore your tiny universe;

who will teach you to share your toys with others;

who will show you the magic of crayons and water colors;

who will teach you to love good books and good music;

who will offer you security through loving discipline;

who will instruct you in rest and in play -

your parents give thanks.

For Jesus said: "Suffer the little children to come unto me, and forbid them not: for of such is the kingdom of God" (Matt. 19:14), and, "Inasmuch as ye have done it unto one of the least of these…ye have done it unto me" (Matt. 25:40 kjv).

God bless those dedicated workers who will occupy such an essential place in your life.

Love, Mom and Dad

Parade of the cousin-Babies

Dear Child,

Each summer for years, your dad and I drove long distances to visit our families. During those visits, we watched, feeling somewhat like outsiders, the endless parade of the cousin-babies.

Gathered at my grandparents' house, my cousins bounced their baby girls and boys on their knees and told us how many words their children could utter. They showed us how many teeth their youngsters had. They informed us of how intelligent he or she was for his or her age. The babies arrived decked out in their best lacy bonnets and matching breeches, polished, white, high-top shoes, and tiny suits and dresses that would have made Shirley Temple jealous.

I must admit, little one, I always enjoyed seeing my cousins each summer, and I especially enjoyed holding their children and hearing all about the latest baby. But I must also admit, I would have been much more excited had I had my own infant to "ooh" and "aah" over.

The decade or more we waited for you seemed much too long to wait, but with your father in college and my full-time job, we didn't see how we could afford a child. I will confess to you, I often felt green with envy when I saw my cousins, as well as my friends, with their own tiny offspring to love and adore.

At times I feared we would wait too long to have children, and that possibly we'd never have a child of our own. During all those years, I wanted a baby more than anything else in the world. The years of college and work seemed to last an eternity.

But, little one, you have changed that picture. With your coming, you will fulfill a long-awaited dream for me.

How I now look forward, with great eagerness, to the visits of the future, when we all gather at my grandparents' house! How much more fun those reunions will be when I have you to hold on my lap, dressed in your Sunday finest, anxious and ready to join the parade of the cousin-babies!

Love, Mom

Memory Makers

Dear Child,

How I look forward to celebrating the holidays with you – Christmas, Easter, birthdays, anniversaries, Mother's Day, Father's Day! We will observe them all and create as much festivity at each as possible.

I especially look forward to my favorite holiday of the year: Christmas. Let me tell you about the wonderful Christmases I had when I was a little girl.

On Christmas morning, my younger sister and I would leap from our beds and run to Mom and Dad's room to wake them up. We dared not go downstairs and peek at the dolls, stuffed animals and games that "Santa" had brought the night before. We wanted to wait and go downstairs together as a family. Mom and Dad, no doubt, planned and worked all year, making dolls' clothes and building play houses to surprise us on Christmas morning.

We hurried our sleepy parents to the living room, and the four of us sat beside the great silver aluminum Christmas tree. We passed out gifts, ripped open boxes, and spent the rest of the morning surrounded by toys, playing happily on the living room floor.

After a hearty breakfast, after the last gift had been put away, after the wrapping paper and empty packages had been carried to the trash, we bathed and dressed. We loaded more brightly wrapped presents into the car and made our way slowly through the light snow to our grandparents' house. We arrived by early afternoon and were greeted by aunts and uncles and cousins, who were also laden with gifts.

My grandmother stayed in the kitchen most of the afternoon, putting the finishing touches on the baked turkey and ham, mashed potatoes and gravy, vegetables (green beans, okra, tomatoes and corn from the past summer's garden), rolls and corn bread, and a freshly-baked pound cake or two. While my mother and my aunts helped my grandmother spread the dinner on the table, my little cousins and I sat around my grandfather as he played his guitar and led us in singing some favorite Christmas carols.

When my grandmother called, "Dinner's ready," the family quickly gathered around the buffet dinner, breathing the combined smells of steaming turkey and cooling cakes, and we recited together the Lord's Prayer or John 3:16. Then my grandfather prayed. He thanked God for his family and for the food we shared. After blessing the food, we eagerly filled our plates high. Some went into the living room to eat, while others sat around the dining room table. My grandmother waited on the buffet sidelines dishing out hot rolls and butter. After everyone had passed through the food line, she walked around, refilling iced-tea glasses and spooning out more corn bread dressing and gravy. I don't believe I ever saw her actually sit down and eat.

After we had eaten, my grandmother urged all of us to sing a song or play the piano or recite a poem. Since we were a rather shy group, my grandmother sometimes had to ask several times before the blushing performer agreed. After a few musical specials, we exchanged presents and thanked the generous givers.

After the dishes were washed and put away, more uncles and aunts sang a song or two. Then each of us said an extended goodbye and talked about the next big get-together we'd enjoy. The end of the joyous day always made me a little bit sad.

Little did I realize how quickly my childhood would pass! Back in those days, I had no idea my grandmother was not really physically able to cook and clean for her family's

Christmas Day – yet she did it! A sickly woman, she gathered her family together for years, putting aside her own health in order to create the Christmas celebration at the wonderful old home place. It was an act of selfless self-giving for which I have always admired her.

I guess in light of the fun and giggles, young children don't stop to think about the one who worked so hard to make it all possible. I now look back and know the love and labor that my grandmother put into each Christmas celebration. She was, indeed, a true memory maker.

I also guess that when young children are surrounded by loving parents and grandparents, uncles, aunts and cousins, they don't think much about all the children in the world who don't have people who love them and so tenderly care for them. Young children, surrounded by large turkeys and all the delicious trimmings, also don't stop to think about all the world's children who don't have food to eat, who don't have the turkeys and trimmings to feast upon. Those thoughts usually visit the minds of grown children – adults – who think back, and with joy and tears, remember the special times.

Those are my special memories, little one. After some years, my grandmother became too feeble to host the great Christmas dinners. For several Christmases after that, our large extended family met for gift exchanging and dessert. Then, as cousins married and had children, the aunts and uncles celebrated the holidays in their own homes with their own immediate families.

During the last ten years or so, for reasons of distance and expense, your dad and I haven't been able to journey back home to our family for Christmas. But each December 25, the memories of Christmas Day with my parents and sister, with my grandparents and other family members, spill forth from my storehouse of treasured remembrances. The celebration, the singing, the family togetherness, the loving and giving, will remain close to my heart as long as I live.

Childhood flees, little one. I pray I can be a memory maker for you. May each holiday we have together be a time of joy

Our Dear Child ✱ ✱ ✱ ✱ ✱

and fun and family love for you to keep and remember long after the day quietly fades away.

And, little child, as I watch the shining magic of future Christmases through your young eyes, may I relive those precious childhood moments spent with my loved ones, and be thankful for the memories of Christmases past.

Love, Mom

Mama's Kitchen

Dear Child,

With pound cakes baking in the oven, and large iron skillets of okra frying on the stove, my grandmother's kitchen was the place to spend long summer afternoons. How well I remember the smells that drifted daily from that kitchen! Mama's fried peach pies alone produced an aroma that would draw me from anywhere at play in the backyard. Between my grandfather's vegetable garden and Mama's cooking, the kitchen remained the center of the household – a gathering spot that made every day so memorable.

Through my childhood, teenage and many of my adult years, Mama's kitchen held an attraction for me. As a small child of two or three, I balanced myself on Mama's hip while she stirred boiling pots of strawberry jelly. How often she would put small bites of steamed cabbage and other niceties in my mouth while I watched!

When my mother and father moved to another state, I couldn't visit my grandparents as often, but each summer I anxiously awaited my two-week vacation at my grandparents' small farm. I would run to the back door and into the kitchen. There Mama would be, making hot fresh vegetable soup or southern corn bread for lunch. Her sink and counter tops stayed laden with mason jars and lids, as well as bountiful ears of corn from the garden, ready to be silked and canned. In spite of the long hours in the kitchen and the hundreds of jars to fill, Mama always had time to stop and talk with her admiring little granddaughter.

The holidays always proved to be happy days at my grandparents' home. Aunts and uncles and grandchildren added to the festivity of the occasion. Again, Mama's kitchen attracted the crowds – the kitchen overflowed with women carrying pans of hot biscuits and large glasses of iced tea. Christmas, Easter, Thanksgiving all proved to be special occasions, but my most precious memories are the everyday dinners. These were the special times when Mama and I, together, sliced tomatoes and onions and cucumbers and talked about growing up and growing old. Those uninterrupted, unscheduled hours, away from the flurry of the rest of the family, were the times I felt free to seek answers to questions that might have embarrassed another granddaughter to mention.

In my searching, no matter how minor the problem, I was always met with thoughtfulness and kindness and understanding. How many times did the pinto beans boil over or the bread burn because Mama stepped away from the stove to talk with me!

I came away from Mama's kitchen with a wealth of knowledge. Unfortunately, I never learned much about cooking, as you will surely notice! I could never match her perfectly-seasoned green beans or creamy coleslaw. But I learned a lot about life in Mama's kitchen. She showed me how to give myself unselfishly to others, how to love those unlovable, how to befriend those who have no friends. Always mindful of others' needs, she showed me how to reach out to all God's children who hurt or need a kind word. Mama taught me how to reach out to God and seek his guidance as I faced some hard growing-up years. I remember Mama most when I stand at my own kitchen sink and reflect on a lifetime of wisdom she shared with me. Her strong Christian faith shone through all that she did, whether caring for others, cooking, or her long hours of grandchild-counseling.

Years have passed since those wonderful days. But sweet smells and sweet memories live on.

I pray that I will have some of Mama's great patience as you, one day, cling to my ankles, as a toddler will, while I struggle to put supper on the table or wash the dishes. May I always recall Mama's patience with me. May Mama's sink-side teaching and wisdom be granted to me, as I try to answer your teenage questions with guiding and caring words. And, little one, may you always feel welcomed, wanted, and loved in my kitchen as, many years ago, I felt in Mama's kitchen.

Love, Mom

Aunt Bessie

Dear Child,

"Aunt Bessie" they all called her, but to me she was "Grammer" until (as she would say) I got "too big for my britches" and didn't want to say Grammer any more. She was an extraordinary ordinary woman. I share her memory with you, little one, in hopes that commingled in your genes will be a measure of her fortitude, faith, and compassion.

My earliest memory of Grammer is of her washing my hands and face over the kitchen sink and singing to me of Jesus and his love. She was incurably religious, a little fanatical to her husband, who was a good man though he never went to church. Grammer did not become a Christian until she turned fifty, but then she got it "whole hog", so to speak.

I remember the summers I spent with her in the country. Every time the church doors were open we were there: Sunday morning, Sunday night, Wednesday night, revivals, homecomings, all day singings. You name it, that church did it, and she saw to it that we didn't miss it!

Much of the Christianity I know and still believe in, I learned from that little old country lady. Illiterate for most of her life, she learned how to read so that she could read the Bible. I'll never forget those late summer evenings, sitting on the front porch, listening to her stumble over the Psalms or stories from the Gospels. Then, before retiring at night, she would kneel down beside her bed and pray for all of us, especially for her son, my dad, who had gone astray, and yes, for her husband to be saved. He never was, so far as I know. I remember wondering how he could withstand so much godliness.

For all her piety and churchgoing, Grammer was best known for her unstinting compassion for anyone in need. No one in our community was ever sick but she was by their side, ready to help, to comfort, to share the loneliness and the hurt. She belonged to the "fellowship of those who bear the mark of pain". No one was ever too low, too poor, too needy for her homespun ministry. Everyone she met was a precious soul for whom Christ died.

I remember the many things Grammer and I did together: picking blackberries in the summer times, walking back home from church on those moonlit, dirt roads, and going to the cemetery every "decoration day" to pay our respects to those who had gone before us.

She died in 1968 when I was a senior in high school. I remember her husband bending over the casket to kiss her goodbye. It's the only time I ever saw him cry. They buried her in the old graveyard overlooking the church. She would have liked that, I think. I miss her terribly, even now. There are times when I would give anything to hear her sing again or just to walk beside her down those country lanes. How I wish she were here to bounce you on her knee and hug you close!

Everyone deserves his or her own personal saint. Grammer was mine.

Love, Dad

Love Doesn't Get Old

Dear Child,

Last night your father and I had an argument about something so insignificant I'd be embarrassed to tell you. We both made unkind comments in less than quiet tones. Silent and sulking, we went to sleep, our conflict unresolved. Today, with little hurts still lingering in the air, we said monotone good mornings and then set out on different schedules.

Why am I telling you this, my little one, who is not yet born, much less able to understand why grown-ups who claim to love each other turn their home into a verbal battlefield over the slightest difference? For precisely that reason. To assure you that even though we sometimes disagree strongly, your father and I do love each other.

Fortunately, we agree on the most problem causing matters: money, sex and religion. The big bugs have all been worked out. But the little bugs? Well, we're still working on those.

Yes, I'll admit, I really do squeeze the toothpaste from the middle rather than the end of the tube. Your father, a longtime toothpaste-tube roller, hates that. But then he leaves the cap off the tube, causing the toothpaste to ooze all over the bathroom sink. That's unpardonable!

And yes, your father does continue to read his book or newspaper when I talk to him. "I can listen to you and read at the same time," he tells me. Nothing makes me madder. So I repeat myself several times, just to make sure he hears me, of course. Then, he legitimately complains that I tell him everything twice!

As you will soon discover, we are both very human. We have our warts, which we cannot always keep hidden. Our marriage, while good, is not perfect; but, little child, please know that the love between your mother and father runs deep. We take our wedding vows seriously. They are not negotiable.

How much easier it would have been for us to disregard those promises and to walk our separate ways during the long school years when money was scarce, living conditions cramped, and immature tempers flared quickly! But we stayed together through those trying times when our union could have so easily dissolved. We planned you for the future when we would be more secure, more settled, and a few years wiser.

On our eleventh wedding anniversary, not long ago, your father gave me a lovely card. The verse inside was simple, yet profound. The thought in the verse was that love doesn't grow old but stronger. What happens to love depends on the individuals. It depends on how they give and receive love.

Little one, you will undoubtedly hear us argue from time to time, as we are both much too stubborn and seldom yield easily to the other's criticisms and demands, but you will be born into a family where love started strong, where love has become stronger through the passing of years. That love, which first began as a heart-fluttering, infatuated passion during our dating and honeymoon days, has since changed into a deep, devoted, genuine affection and concern for each other. We have worked hard to make our marriage a solid one, to make a comfortable, peaceful, loving nest for you – a visible, breathing symbol of our love.

Love doesn't get old; it gets better, it gets richer, it gets stronger, it gets….

Love, Mom

5. What in the world are you coming to?

★ ★ ★ ★ ★

"A baby is God's opinion that the world should go on."
Carl Sandburg

A Great Big Beautiful World

Dear Child,

Soon you will open your eyes to a great big beautiful world. In the spring and summer the robin's song will awaken you. In your own backyard, you will discover the bright glow of the red azalea bush that blooms early each spring, the rough bark of the giant oak tree that towers over the porch, and the clean smell of new grass just mowed. Fall will gently brush you with cool evening breezes. It will excite you with an array of red, orange and yellow leaves falling from the trees. Winter will plant bountiful memories of a toasty fire, warm hot chocolate, and a cold nose and cheeks as you bundle up and play outside in the snow.

With the change of each season, the world comes alive with new excitement. As if for the first time, we see, hear, smell, touch, taste, walk in, talk about and marvel at the freshness and beauty of nature.

But God, in his infinite wisdom, created nature so that all could enjoy it. To those who cannot see the beauty and majesty of a rose, he gave velvet petals for them to touch; to those who cannot hear the soft sprinkle of a summer rain, he gave the fragrance of cleansed earth and air for them to smell; to those who cannot touch the round firmness of a ripe apple, he gave a delicate flavor for them to taste; and to those who cannot speak the words of adoration, he gave soft, furry puppies who need no words to know they're loved.

Love, Mom and Dad

God - The Mystery

Dear Child,

He who says, I believe in God, says more than he can justify,
more than he knows, more even than he senses or suspects; he says
that God's reality is more real than his own life, that God is nearer
than hands and feet, that He is the most sublime, but also the most
common, that He is a God 'in heaven above and on earth below,' the
furthest away and the closest at hand, the unattainable One, who
was already nearby us before we were born.

Gerardus Van Der Leeuw

I don't remember the first time I heard the word "God", nor
what I imagined it must have meant. It will likely be the same
with you. It's a simple word – God. Not hard to say, spell or
write on a page. It's a common, everyday word. Everybody
uses it, either in vain or in prayer, to poke fun or to give
thanks. Doubtless, you will hear it a lot. So I thought I should
try to tell you who God is, or rather what God means for me.

The first word that comes to mind is "mystery". Some
people know too much about God. They speak about him
with such certainty and familiarity, with no sense of distance
and with little genuine respect. God is their cosmic buddy,
their heavenly Chum, the "Man Upstairs," always available,
always at their beck and call. Too often we merely worship
a God created in our own image, made up of our collective
wishes of what God ought to be.

For me, God has been most real in moments of deep
mystery – moments of beauty or sorrow, moments of

exhilaration, pain or insight. I remember two such moments vividly. Once, after your mother and I had spent the night in a sleepy little town, we got up very early in the morning hoping to make our destination before that nightfall. But in the midst of ordinary travel, we drove headlong into the realm of breathtaking beauty. High in the mountains, we drove slowly along the winding road, the fog nestling deep in the crevices, the sun just breaking forth and rising over the powdered peaks. It was absolutely gorgeous. I understood completely what a friend of mine meant when he once said, "The reason I became a Christian was because I knew there had to be someone to say 'thank you' to."

On a quite different occasion, I was sitting on the front pew of a country church that was tightly packed for the funeral of my grandmother. There, seized by a moment shaped by death, trying to choke out the words of a hymn, I was brought face to face with Him who claimed to be life, even in the midst of death. Grasping for a God who seemingly was nowhere to be found, I discovered in my grief and loss a Presence hitherto unknown.

The second word I would use is "sovereign". We could say the Almighty, omnipotent, absolute, ultimate, the ground of Being: all of these "attributes" of God, as we call them, simply mean that finally, when all is said and done, God will be God. No person, power, being or force either will or can conquer him.

This is what the Bible means when it refers to God as the Lord. God is the Lord of time and space, heaven and earth, the past, present and future. "It is he that hath made us and not we ourselves," said the psalmist (Ps. 100:3 KJV). This means that we – all of us – are totally, absolutely dependent on God. He is the source of our life and of all life.

The third word is "love". God is love. Love is not just something God does; it is that which God is. His mystery and his sovereignty are clothed in infinite love and holiness. We see this most clearly in Jesus, who told his disciples: "He who has seen me has seen the Father," and "I and the Father are one." (John 14:9 and 10:30 NASB).

Without Jesus we could perhaps sense something of God's power and mystery; we could look up at the stars and marvel at the beauty of creation; we could hear the rushing wind and tremble at the awesome power of nature. But Jesus gives God a face, a face we can see and touch, a face which can look into our deepest hurts and call us to forgiveness and grace.

God is the mystery of sovereign and holy love, revealed fully in the face of Christ. I think that is the best I can do. Of course, it isn't good enough. None of our words ever are. An old confession of faith says that we human beings were created "to love God and enjoy him forever". If we could capture God in our words or ideas, then our enjoyment of him would not last very long, certainly not forever.

Remember this: the very God who in the secret depths of his own will brought us into being, has determined that we shall live with him and enjoy his presence, both in this life and throughout eternity. This same God will see to it that it shall be so.

Love, Dad

Reverence for Life

Dear Child,

Last night I bent over your mother's bulging body and listened to the strong beating of your little heart. You are alive! How many fathers before me must have listened with bated breath to those muted sounds and rejoiced at the miracle of new life sloshing, palpitating, eager to announce its imminent advent? Surely the psalmist must have had some such experience when he prayed: "For you created my inmost being; you knit me together in my mother's womb. I praise you because I am fearfully and wonderfully made; your works are wonderful, I know that full well" (Ps. 139:13-14).

You are alive and you are unique. There never has been one quite like you before; there will never be another quite like you again. Already you possess your own distinctive genetic code, your particular mix of chromosomes and DNA molecules, even your own fingerprints. Already you are a human person. To be sure, you are entrusted to our care, especially your mother's, in these special months of gestation, but you are ours only in a provisional sense. We do not own you. We have only been permitted to parent you, to welcome you into this world, to give you – we hope – a helpful boost on your journey which has already begun.

You are unique, but you are not alone. You will enter a world filled with all kinds of other living creatures. All of life is sacred because it comes from God. We humans have sometimes acted as if we were the only living creatures on earth, as though we had no responsibility for our fellow creatures, or even for the biosphere that sustains both their life and ours. Albert Schweitzer once wrote that it is our duty to share and maintain life. He said that reverence concerning all life is the greatest commandment in its most elementary form.

Several years ago we watched with amazement as the first pictures of earth were relayed back to our planet from astronauts circling the moon. It was eerie and wonderful all at the same time, to see that blue-green orb floating in the dark immensity of space, to know that all of us are fellow travelers on Spaceship Earth, which, so far as we can tell, is the only habitat of life within this vast universe. We listened to the astronauts read those haunting words from Genesis 1:31: "And God saw everything that he had made, and behold, it was very good."(KJV)

All of life is good, because God made it. Never treat with contempt or carelessness any living thing. Tiny kittens, big whales, puffy white dandelions, jonquils, azaleas, every blade of grass, even the snowflake with its own intricate design – like you, each of these is unique and has a place in God's wonderful world.

The society that awaits you, little one, often places a limited value on life, even on human life. Sometimes it is expendable altogether – whether it be the as yet unborn, for whom, like Jesus, there is no room, whose coming might crowd the space of those already here; the senior citizen who has outlived his usefulness; or the mentally impaired whose contributions to society are limited by disability.

The greatest moral issues of our day are issues of life and death. If we are to survive as a civilization, as a global community, then we must recover a reverence for life. Perhaps the best advice I can give you is: walk lightly on this good earth. Mistreat neither animal nor fellow human, for we both inhale the same fresh air. Take enough, but not too much, of earth's precious bounty; it is yours to borrow, not to possess. Leave something for your neighbors and the yet unborn. Live kindly with all creatures, the horned and webbed, the scaled and finned, the feathered and skinned; they too have a right to be here. And remember the words of Cecil Alexander:

> All things bright and beautiful,
> All creatures great and small,
> All things wise and wonderful,
> The Lord God made them all.

Love, Dad

Peacemaking

Dear Child,

I remember the day Pope John Paul II was shot. Your mother and I were returning from – of all places – a monastery: a religious community, a place of tranquility and peace, where men pray and work and spend their days in the worship of God. The horrible news came across the car radio; someone had shot the Pope.

We were shocked and afraid; afraid for the Pope, afraid for our friends, the monks, whose world would be shattered by the awful news, afraid for ourselves, and yes, afraid for you, weighing heavy now at six months in your journey toward birth.

The world is pregnant with violence: assassinations, coups d'état, invasions, wars and rumors of wars. None of us is exempt. We think we are secure, insulated from the cruelty and pain we see portrayed each evening on the network news; in just such a moment we are apt to become the victims of a careless driver crazed by drink or of a burglar with a pistol in his hand.

We have often asked ourselves, along with countless other couples: "Do we want to bring a new, helpless life into this violent world?" Of course, there has always been violence, ever since Cain – the first baby born into the world – rose up in anger and slew his brother Abel – the second baby born into the world. But now it is different, very different. You will belong to the second generation born after the explosion of the first nuclear bombs. You will grow up under the shadow of an ominous mushroom cloud. For the first time in history, the human race has the capacity to destroy itself: sui-genocide.

I read recently of school children in New Hampshire, who, aware of this threat, doubted if the world would survive long enough for them to become adults. When I was a little boy we wondered what we would be when we grew up: lawyer, doctor, ballplayer; now children discuss not what they will be, but whether they will be.

I wish I could protect you from all of this, somehow. Yet I know that I cannot, not for long anyway. To be alive is to be vulnerable. To be human is to be susceptible to hurt, even violence. Why, then, have we decided, deliberately, with considerable forethought, to take the risk of becoming parents?

Because we believe that life is better than death, love is stronger than hate, and that, despite the evil around us, there is a goodness within us – and within you – which calls us to wholeness and peace even in the midst of violence and fear. We have decided to say "yes" to life, to God and to you, because we believe the risk is worth it, and because you too should have your own chance to say "yes".

God, too, chose to send his child into a violent world. Indeed, his birth was the occasion of horrible violence, the slaughter of the innocent babies of Bethlehem. In the end, Jesus himself was a victim of this world's cruel vengeance. Yet he had a way of living and hoping, of smiling and laughing, crying and loving, so that little children found him irresistible, tarnished women were made pure by his embrace, and lepers found cleansing and acceptance in his touch. He was a healer, a forgiver, a peacemaker. The motto of his life was: "Do not resist one who is evil" (Matt. 5:39).

The life of nonresistance is not the path of least resistance. It requires enormous courage; it implies incalculable risk. It does not mean acquiescence in the face of evil, but rather resistance of a higher order: the resistance of love which conquers fear. So that in the end Jesus could pray: "Father, forgive them; …Father, into thy hands I commend my spirit." (Luke 23:34, 46 KJV).

✱ ✱ ✱ ✱ ✱ What in the World Are You Coming To?

As you enter this shaky, scary world, dear little one, I pray for you an inner serenity, a peace that the world neither gives nor takes away.

Love, Dad

World Hunger

Dear Child,

With a cup of sugared and creamed coffee and my second apple Danish in hand, I began to read Ronald Sider's book, *Rich Christians in an Age of Hunger*. I was to lead a devotional service that week, and since that particular month had been set aside by my denomination for an emphasis on world hunger, I had chosen that topic for my devotion.

Two hours later I closed the book. I felt numb, ashamed and somewhat in shock. I couldn't believe what I had read: "Millions die each year of starvation." "One billion people have stunted bodies or damaged brains because of inadequate food." And being in my present condition, the statistic that spoke the loudest to me was: "In developing countries, one child in four dies before the age of five, and half of these deaths are related to inadequate diets!"

One child in four!

The scales had finally dropped from my eyes. I "crawled out of my cave" and, for the first time, through the eyes of Ronald Sider, I could actually "see" the frail, bloated and diseased bodies of those dying of starvation – little babies who were unable to seek food for themselves, who lay sick and dying from malnourishment.

I reflected on my day. The hearty breakfast and supper, the numerous in-between-meal snacks, the hamburger I had gobbled down for lunch – I had had my usual orgy with food. Driving through town, I had been tempted by huge fried chicken dinners on billboards, steaming sausage and biscuit posters in windows, and pickles, lettuce and onions dripping off double-cheeseburgers on outdoor menus. I had been enticed with a cackle, grunt and moo on every corner!

All the while, the radio jingle shouted: "Aren't you h-u-n-g-r-y?" Moments later, only halfway home, I could stand it no longer. I succumbed to the pleasure of two scoops of fudge ice cream that I had painstakingly selected from among thirty other flavors. I knew I would have to diet off those extra calories, but I didn't care. Next time I would eat low-calorie ice cream.

I realized with much anguish that while I stuffed myself on food all day, 10,000 people had died of starvation and hunger-related diseases.

I felt guilty. And rightly so. What had I done to help feed the hungry people of the world? Nothing. How could I have been so blind for so many years? How could I have stood on the sidelines while the world's mothers hoped and prayed that their infants would have enough milk for the next day?

Little child, your mother feels ashamed. You will probably never know the pangs of hunger. We might never have abundant luxuries, but we will always have adequate food on our table. As a Christian, as a mother-to-be, I feel convicted to help those who are starving in the world. An inner voice tugs at me: "People are still starving this very moment. What are you going to do about the world's hunger now?"

Little child, I pray that God will haunt me with the sunken eyes of dying men and women, burden me with a baby's unanswered cry for milk, and direct me in ways that I can help to put food into the mouths of starving people.

And that, little one, is a dangerous prayer.

Love, Mom

Love Versus Hate

Dear Child,

I read today of a sixteen-year-old boy accused of murdering black demonstrators in North Carolina. He had tagged along with his parents, the newspaper said, when they attended Ku Klux Klan rallies. His mother had sent him to school with Nazi arm bands around his sleeves. Yesterday five people were killed, and a sixteen-year-old boy stood among the accused. A young life, seared by hate, ruined perhaps beyond repair.

Little one, along with your fair white skin you will inherit a position of privilege and respect in our culture. But you will also inherit a history of prejudice, bigotry, slavery, segregation, racism and discrimination. As a race, we white people have much to repent of, much to make up for.

Growing up in the Southern States of America in the turbulent sixties, I remember the ugly slurs, the condescending gestures, rear seats reserved for blacks, schools which were separate but never equal, water fountains and rest rooms divided by race.

Somehow, even then, I knew it was wrong. It was wrong for the blacks to resort to violence. Yes, but it was equally wrong for the whites who claimed to be Christian to tolerate the conditions that provoked the violence.

I hope that you will be spared some of the prejudices I had to overcome. The racism of this generation seems not as overt or blatant as in my generation, but it is still there, smoothed over by polite niceties perhaps, but ready to erupt at a moment's notice.

I hope that we can instill within you ideals that leave no room for bigotry: belief in the inherent dignity of every person; fairness and quality for all peoples; appreciation for diverse cultures and traditions. In the final analysis, you must decide for yourself what role you will play in the ongoing struggle for racial justice. Remember, dear one, that Jesus Christ came to set all peoples free.

Love, Dad

Jealousy or Gratitude?

Dear Child,

You are probably going to get a lot of advice from me, and I hope most of it will be worth your heeding. But I am sure about this one: don't ever be jealous of anyone else.

Growing up, you will doubtless be confronted with many situations in which you may be tempted to be jealous. We live in a culture that cultivates competition and you will soon know what this means: on the sports field, in the drama club, even in church youth circles. The Bible says that "its jealousy unyielding as the grave" (Song 8:6) Jealousy was even present among Jesus' first disciples. They argued among themselves about who would receive the greatest glory, about who would be most in the limelight in Jesus' new kingdom.

When we are jealous of someone else, whoever it is, we are saying in effect, "Lord, you made a big mistake in creating me. Why didn't you give me his gifts? Why didn't you make me like her?"

Instead of always looking over our shoulder at someone else, we can be glad that God has created us and gifted us in the special way that no one else can ever duplicate. What is the opposite of jealousy? It is gratitude. It is to say with an open, thankful heart: "Thank you, Lord, for being the kind of God you are, for making me and calling me to serve you and to love you just as I am, with all of my warts and faults and shortcomings. I know you have a purpose for my life. Help me to live with joy and thanksgiving every single day."

Love, Dad

The Meaning of Friendship

Dear Child,

We have some special friends that your mother and I made when we lived far from home. The winters in that far-away city were long and cold and lonely. We were students, and had little money with which to celebrate the holidays.

I think it was during our second year there that we met this extraordinary older couple. We came to know them and love them, and even though our ages were far apart, we found we had much in common. We decided to adopt one another. They would become our stand-in parents, and we their stand-in children.

Thanksgivings, Christmases, birthdays: we shared so many wonderful occasions together. They both had hearts brimming with compassion. I remember singing carols around the piano, playing long games of Scrabble by the fireplace, holding hands for prayer around the dinner table, sitting together at dusk, savoring the stillness and our love for each other.

Our friends have gone to be with Jesus now. We miss them, but we have many happy memories of times spent together. They taught us the meaning of deep friendship. A friend is someone who accepts you as you are, no matter what; who stands beside you through good times and bad; who receives the gift of your love and returns it to you with no conditions. Friends are gifts from God to heal our lonely hearts.

Love, Dad

On Being a christian

Dear Child,

When I was just a little boy, four or five years old, I declared one day that when I grew up I was going to be a preacher! This statement prompted my uncle to ask: "Are you going to be a Baptist preacher or a Mormon preacher?" As a young man, my uncle had converted to Mormonism. He spent the rest of his life trying to convert everybody else. One of the most vivid memories of my childhood is of long summer evenings sitting on my uncle's front porch, slapping at mosquitoes, and talking religion.

"Why are you a Baptist?" he would ask. "Don't you want to belong to the true church, the church founded by Jesus?" Those front-porch seminars were an important part of my religious education. I was forced to examine my beliefs and my tradition. Sometimes it seemed the foundations beneath me were shaking, but in the end I emerged a stronger and better Christian.

Sooner or later someone will probably ask you the same question my uncle put to me: "Why are you a Baptist?" "Why are you a Christian?" You will have to formulate your own answer. What follows are some of my thoughts, which I hope will be of help in your own struggles.

I am a Christian before I am a Baptist. Within the whole family of God there are many diverse groupings, some with very ancient traditions, others relatively recent in origin. Every person who follows Jesus Christ as Lord is our spiritual cousin, no matter his church affiliation. With them we are united in one common faith. That which binds us together – our oneness in Christ – is infinitely greater than those things which pull us apart.

I am a Baptist because it was from Baptists that I first received the gospel. As a very young child, I was taken to a Baptist Sunday School and church. Through the singing, preaching, teaching and warmth I experienced there, I learned about God's great love revealed in Jesus Christ. In time I came to claim the tradition in which I was nurtured as my own.

I cannot bequeath my faith to you. Religion, like measles, is better "caught" than "taught". I hope that you will catch the spirit of Jesus' love for you in the way your mother and I will love you. I hope you will catch a sense of the wonder and mystery of God as we worship together as a family, as we walk together through the woods on autumn days, as we celebrate Advent and Christmas and Easter. John Baillie, a great theologian, once remarked that even as a five-year-old boy he realized that his parents answered to a higher authority. I want you to know that our family answers to a higher authority too.

I promise never to demand more from you than you are willing and able to give. I will not quash your questions, nor stifle your doubts before they have had a chance to surface. A faith that has not been buffeted by doubts is not likely to be a very strong faith. Be sensitive to your doubts and to your conscience, but learn somehow to doubt your doubts too, and to know that no Christian has anything to fear from the truth.

I will not expect you to agree with me. I may argue with you, try to persuade you, even sometimes get mad at you for not seeing the light as clearly as I see it. But when all is said and done, I know that a sacred, inviolate covenant exists between you and God: "soul competency," someone once called it. I will respect your integrity as a person, as a child of God. I may not agree with you, but I will always love you and respect you.

Why am I a Christian? Because, ultimately, the grace of God has come to me in Jesus Christ. It has taken me by surprise, it has brought meaning and purpose to my life, or perhaps better, it has taught me that the only meaning and purpose there is in life is to know God, to enjoy him and to love him forever.

I pray that you will catch this grace, and be caught by it.

Love, Dad

Life After Life

Dear Child,

Surrounded in my early childhood with elderly adults, I first learned about death while still a small boy. My great-great aunt died when I was just three or four. One of my earliest memories is of her wake and funeral. Then there was another aunt, and an uncle, and then my father, all of whom died before I had become a teenager. Sooner or later everyone has to face the reality of death.

So far as we know, of all the species on earth, only human beings can anticipate their own death. Like all living creatures, we too must die; but unlike any other living creature, we know this. We think about it, expect it, and plan for it. The burden of this foreknowledge can be intolerable. But it need not be so, for death is also a part of life, and the gateway to a mystery greater and more wonderful than anything we have known before.

Why do people die? That question is as old as the human race. To answer it completely would be to remove in large measure the mystery of death. There is something tragic about death, despite our modern efforts to smother its ugliness in perfumed funeral parlors filled with freshly-cut flowers. The Bible teaches that death is linked with sin (Rom. 6:23). It is an enemy to be overcome (1 Cor. 15:26), a bondage from which we must be freed. To be sure, death can also be a release, as when someone has suffered for long years with no relief. But there lingers within us all the suspicion, the hope, the whisper of life after death, the "intimation of immortality" as Wordsworth called it.

Where are those who have died? Christians believe that Jesus' death and resurrection has decisively affected our own destiny. Paul admonishes us not to sorrow as those who have no hope (1 Thess. 4:13), for to be absent from the body is to be present with the Lord (2 Cor. 5:8). "With the Lord": that's the only sure answer we have when we stand at the graveside of a loved one, when our grief is more than we can bear – they're with the Lord, in his presence, in his care, enfolded in his infinite comfort.

So what is it like to die? Suppose I could somehow get your attention, little one, make you understand me, as you are now in your mother's womb. Suppose I were to say to you: "Dear little one, in a few weeks you are going to be born. A life of excitement, joy and love beyond anything you have known awaits you on this side of birth." Yet you respond: "I don't want to be born. I like it in here. I'm warm, I'm comfortable. All of my needs are being met. I've never been born before. I'm afraid to be born."

But then you are born. You discover a wonderful world of color and sound, of music, toys and friends, a mom and dad who love you more than anything else in the world, and you think: "Oh, this is so much better than before."

The years go by, you grow up, get married, have children of your own, eventually even grandchildren. Life is good. Then one day you notice a gray hair in the mirror, your step is a little slower, your memory is not quite as quick as once it was, and you realize, "I'm going to die. I don't want to die. I've never died before. I love this world, my family and friends, my work. Why must I leave them now?"

But then you die. Suddenly you discover: "Why, this is wonderful. It's just like being born!"

Jesus said: "I am the resurrection and the life. He who believes in me will live, even though he dies; and whoever lives and believes in me will never die" (John 11:25).

Love, Dad

To Be a Pilgrim

Dear Child,

One of the great metaphors of the Christian life, both in the Bible and throughout Christian history, is that of a journey. God called Abraham and Sarah to leave their comfortable life back in Ur of the Chaldees and to venture forth on a journey to a place they had never been before. The children of Israel were miraculously delivered by God from slavery in Egypt, but they had a long journey ahead of them before they reached the Promised Land. Jonah was a reluctant journeyman, running away from God, or trying to, until he could no longer flee from the destination God had mapped out for him. Much later, John Bunyan told a story of Christian, a man who set out on a pilgrimage toward that Shining City whose builder and maker is God.

I believe that you too will be a pilgrim, and that your entire life will be a journey that will never end until you rest in the arms of God. I don't know where your spiritual journey will take you, but I hope you will find good, faithful friends to walk alongside you, to share your burdens, and to help keep you focused on the goal you are heading for.

Pilgrims are not tourists. Tourists travel about hither and yon, looking for adventure, trying to find excitement, thrills, and new experiences, like a bee darting from one flower to the next, never satisfied, never resting. St. Augustine once said, "Oh Lord, our hearts are restless until they find their rest in You." But pilgrims are different. A true pilgrim will not be distracted by the conditions of the road or the circumstances of his travels. A pilgrim has a destination, a goal, a purpose. The pilgrim hears the sounds of another world and he journeys steadfastly, even if sometimes on stumbling feet, toward the City of God.

The Bible says that Abraham and Sarah died before they reached that city; but they never stopped longing for it, yearning for it, waiting and looking for it with eager anticipation. So may it be with you, little pilgrim.

Love, Dad

6. As the Time Draws Near

★ ★ ★ ★ ★

"Our soul waiteth for the Lord." (Ps. 33:20 KJV)

With Hope for the Spawning

Dear Child,

"With hope for the spawning," wrote a friend on the flyleaf of his new novel when we asked him to autograph our copy. The basis for this hopeful wish is, on one level, obvious: your mother's bulging belly, laden with child, and no longer able to be so easily camouflaged by gathered skirts and fulsome blouses. You are now many months in the making, and there is no hiding that!

To spawn: to hatch, to make, to procreate, produce, parent, to engender, to generate, to bring into existence. In the beginning, the Bible says, the Spirit of God brooded over the mystery of the primordial dark, and the world which had never been was somehow spawned. Now, deep inside the darkness of your mother's womb, felt but unseen, you too are struggling to arrive, to become.

I see the signs of your imminent *parousia* and think of hope; "the thing with feathers that perches in the soul," Emily Dickinson called it. So illusory and fragile, so easily ruffled and destroyed. Maybe the ancient Hebrews were more accurate when they chose for hope a word which means literally: a cord, a rope, an attachment. Hope is that which binds us to the future; it is our link to life, and to God.

And you – in process, in transit, in spawning, here but not yet here – you, by your fragile presence, have called forth hope. You are the cord which binds us to the promise, and so we hope, as parents ever have hoped, that with your advent we might make a new beginning of our own fractured selves;

that you will give us the gift of beginning again; that for you the wrinkles will be fewer and farther in between; that in a world which seems sometimes to be an "an orphan's home", you will find a surer answer than we to the poet's query: "Shall we never have peace without sorrow?"

Perhaps these are only half-hopes built on half-truths. Forgive us when we try to impose our own dreams upon you. Be a little patient if we hold on to you too tightly. There is pain and promise enough for all of us to share.

You have come to us as a gift. We celebrate your spawning and wait with tiptoed eagerness to see what God is up to this time!

Love, Dad

Letting Go

Dear Child,

You are now existing in my safe, small world. Your nest is the womb – warm, comfortable, inviolate. No one can harm you unless they harm me first. Wherever I go, you go with me. You are nestled secure within my shelter, protected by my frame, sustained by my nourishment, close to my heart.

But one day very soon, you will leave my protective body. We will labor together: I to be liberated, you to be born. I must watch you gasp for your first breaths of life, knowing I will be helpless in your struggle to survive the early moments in the world. Once you depart from my body, I must begin letting go of you. You will emerge independent of me.

You will depend on me less and less as you develop, especially as you grow to adulthood. I must watch you stumble and fall as you struggle to walk. As you learn to feed yourself, I must allow you to become frustrated. As you play with others, I must let you protect yourself from the larger children. How hard is this letting go! How much easier it would be to keep you close within me!

I empathize with the new mother bird who must push her fledging baby from its nest, as nature dictates. If she ruled her actions by heart rather than by instinct, how different her decision might be. She might worry: is my little one old enough to test his wings? What if he cannot fly well enough to keep from dashing his frail body against the ground? Who will come to his rescue if he is not yet able to protect himself from predators?

As an expectant mother, I already express similar fears: when will you be old enough to climb the stairs, play outside alone, cross the street unassisted? What if I give you too much freedom, too soon, and you are hurt? Who will protect you from a dangerous world when I am not near?

Little one, how can I let go of you? Am I strong enough to allow you to suffer "for your own good"? Can I stand by while you make mistakes in order to "learn from your experiences"? I will feel each pain you suffer, each error of your judgment.

I pray that I will not be an overprotective mother, never allowing you to grow up, to take responsibility for yourself, or to become an independent adult. Dear one, I will let go of you. I accept this difficult challenge that will one day face me. I promise you your right to freedom, freedom to choose and freedom to experience, no matter how hard letting go of you will be.

Love, Mom

oh! The Horror stories!

Dear Child,

When I was a little girl, I loved to go to slumber parties. A group of us constant gigglers gathered overnight at one of our homes, wrapped up in warm pajamas, and ate ice cream and cake until we felt sick. Then, around midnight, each girl told her most spine-tingling horror story.

Seated in a circle on the floor, with all the lights off, we heard tales of ghosts and goblins and never-to-be-explained phenomena. The storyteller "oohed" and "aahed" at just the right moments, pointed her finger at the scared listeners, and assured each of us that "this really did happen – it's a true story!"

When the tale proved particularly terrifying, the story-teller forced us to hear the details over and over. Opening her eyes wide, and using ever-increasing sound effects and hand gestures, she made the story grow ten times scarier with each repetition.

How I loved those parties and ice cream! But how I loathed the horror stories! The goblins stayed with me long after I returned home. They caused many sleepless, closet-checking nights.

As I grew older, the slumber parties ceased, and the horror stories became a thing of the past – that is, until I became pregnant! Then, suddenly, I discovered that every woman who had ever had a baby, who had ever almost had a baby, or who had a friend who had thought about having a baby, had a spine-tingling tale of the pregnancy, labor and delivery to tell me.

My noticeably round belly has made me the direct target of every veteran mother's war story: her childbirth drama. The storytellers "ooh" and "aah" at just the right moment, point their fingers at the scared listener – me! – and assure me that "this really did happen – it's a true story!" Each time they repeat the dreadful details, I sense their travail has grown tenfold.

Oh! The horror stories! Everywhere I go, I encounter ghosts and goblins and never-to-be-explained phenomena! The grocery store checkout clerk: "How sweet, you're going to have a baby! Oh, oh, my poor daughter just lost her baby. Only three months pregnant, too. That happens quite often, you know. Now how far along are you?"

A city bus passenger: "You say you're six months pregnant? My dear, you certainly seem small to be six months along. I'd certainly check with my doctor to see what's wrong. My niece was small like you are – God rest her soul!"

The beauty-shop hair washer: "Good luck to you when you have that baby! My baby came a whole month late. I got huge! And my labor lasted seventy-two hours. Thought I'd die. I'll never go through that again!"

The classic comment came at a bookstore as I stood, full figured, thumbing through a book entitled *Childbirth*. A woman I had never met walked up to me, looked me straight in the eye, screwed up her face in a painful contortion, and proclaimed: "It'll hurt! No matter what you read – it'll hurt!"

Oh! The horror stories! And even worse, the old, silly tales, which have been passed on to expectant mothers for hundreds of years.

"Sleep at night with one light bright or your child will be born with bad eyesight."

"Pajamas put on left foot last will bury sins of ancestors past."

"Enter thy slumber chamber on right and save your child from a fateful plight."

Is escape not possible? Everywhere I go, someone has a story to tell me, or a tale to warn me, or a word of advice to share with me. And they scare me beyond words!

Little child, I have no particular ending to this letter to you. The horror stories will no doubt stop only after you are born. Until that time, I will try to ignore them. I'll pay no attention to the horror stories or tales.

I'm tired tonight. The day has been long. I'll turn on the kitchen light and go to my bedroom, put on my pajamas left foot last, glance in the mirror then look at my mother's picture and climb into bed – on the right side, of course!

Love, Mom

As Time Grows Near

Dear Child,

As the time grows very near to your birth, I grow very nervous. You are my firstborn. I look forward to your arrival with both excitement and fear.

I lie on my bed at night and wonder: "Will this be the night?" I must confess to you, the thought of the delivery – of our being thrust into the unknown – causes me much concern. Will your birth be painful for me? Am I physically strong enough to withstand the discomfort I've so often heard mothers describe?

But even more important than myself, my thoughts turn to you. Will you be strong enough to endure the long hours of labor? I have seen the newborns in maternity ward windows – the little heads misshapen, the tiny faces swollen and bruised. Could it be that labor is harder on the baby than on the mother? At least an adult can better understand what is happening.

As the time grows close, do you, little one, also realize the nearness of your birth? Do you fear it? Are you so safe and warm and comfortable within me that you dread your entrance into a cold and alien world?

I think back to my mother and to her mother, and to her mother – to generations of mothers around the world in days gone by, who have felt this universal anxiety about the birth of their first child. If only those feelings could be put adequately into words, perhaps mothers-to-be of the future could look upon their child's birth with fewer fears.

Our Dear Child ✱ ✱ ✱ ✱ ✱

My thoughts travel to another mother, in another time, in another part of the world. After a long and tiring journey, unable to find rest in the crude lodging, with no one near to give her medical attention, she delivered her firstborn. I believe God was close by her, giving her the needed strength on that night in a stable nearly two thousand years ago. And, little one, I believe he will be just as close to us, giving us the needed strength as together we embark on the advent of your birth.

That, dear child, will be my prayer for you – and for me.

Love, Mom

May We Be Good Parents

Dear Child,

We pray that by working lovingly and hard together, your mother and I may be good parents to you. Having had no experience in this line of work, we hope you will have infinite patience with us. Excuse our slow and clumsy hands as we pick you up and lay you down. Try to understand when we lean over your crib and gaze at you, scratching our heads, both of us puzzled as to why you cry. Forgive your proud parents when we dress you up in uncomfortable (but cute) buttons and bows to show you off to our friends and family.

You will come into this world a helpless human being, completely dependent on your mother and me for your very life. What an awesome responsibility for two such green parents! Aside from keeping you fed, clean, warm and safe, we will have much to teach you about yourself and about life. We pray that we may learn all we can about your bodily maintenance from the baby books and then put them aside, allowing our basic common sense to take over.

May we show you unlimited love, for a child who is loved will show love to others. May we treat you with kindness, for a child who is treated with kindness will be kind to others. May we show you respect, for a child who is respected at home will respect those around him. And may we teach you the value of life, for a child who is taught that life has value, will value the lives of others.

This, little one, is our prayer for you.

Love, Dad

You're Late!

Dear Child,

They said you would be here by August 30. It's now September 10. You're late! What are you waiting for? How will you ever learn to be punctual when you can't even arrive on time?

This is the hardest part of all – the waiting. The doctor says there's nothing to do but just wait. In God's own good time, he says, you will come. Not to worry. Tell that to your mother! She's so gigantically pregnant already, I think she will explode if it's much longer. And me – I have classes to teach, appointments to keep, things to do. How can I do anything when all of life is on hold, waiting for you?

I guess people always have to wait for something. The postman, vacation, payday, the phone to ring, church to let out, retirement, the doctor, even death sometimes. Much of life is lived in the waiting zone.

So here I sit. Nothing to do but wait. Everything's ready: nursery's set up; route to the hospital memorized; list in my coat pocket of people to call once you're born. Nothing to do but wait. Would you mind hurrying up, huh?

Love, Dad

7. Arrival - Happy Birthday!

★ ★ ★ ★ ★

*"You brought me forth from my mother's womb.
I will ever praise you."* (Ps. 71:6)

On Birth's Day

Dear Child,

Our day has arrived! Finally! Since Mother Nature has delayed the event some two weeks, our doctor has decided to step ahead of her and medically induce the labor.

Last night, I frantically packed our suitcase, getting ready for the big day: nightgowns, robes and slippers for me; a pink embroidered baby blouse and lace socks for you. (You will be a fitly dressed Alyce Elizabeth, to be sure, but with the pink and the lace, you will be a somewhat feminine-looking son!)

I went to bed. I got up. I checked and rechecked my case. I went back to bed. The telephone rang. I jumped up to answer it. Our minister's wife wanted to send her best wishes. I went back to bed for the third time, but sleep would not come. Ten, eleven, twelve o'clock – I lay awake all night, the victim of excited anticipation. I shut off the alarm before it loudly announced six o'clock!

Birth's Day is finally here. I jump out of bed, this time with reason. Our day has arrived, little child. I look down and say to you, "This is it." "No turning back, no turning back," as the old hymn goes.

Your dad and I dress quickly, add the wet toothbrush to my bag and get into the car. Oh, it's so early – six thirty in the morning! The streets are empty of cars. I notice the kitchen lights in neighborhood homes just beginning to faintly glow as sleepy inhabitants stumble to their coffee pots. The damp, early September morning air smells sweet. We sit silently, both of us in deepest thought, as we drive to the place where we will first be introduced to each other as parent and child.

We lock the car and walk slowly into the hospital entrance. Before I can be rolled to my room by wheelchair, an unnecessary product of procedure, we must first fill out sheets and sheets of forms: Social Security numbers, insurance card identifications, addresses, zip codes.

I turn and ask Timothy, "Who can think of such mundane matters on a day like this?"

"Procedure," the nurse tells me.

The next hour is a whirl of activity. More forms to sign, examinations, injections, X-rays, then the doctor reports the news. He tells me you are in breech position and must be delivered by Caesarean section. Shock! I did not expect to hear that news.

"But wait," I inwardly protest. "I was looking forward to the birth some ten to twelve hours from now. I need that time to further prepare myself for the meeting."

A little voice within me chuckles and tells me I have had a full nine months to prepare for this meeting!

"But," I continue quietly, "what about those six weeks of LaMaze classes to prepare us for natural childbirth? The hours of instruction, the weeks of breathing practice to make childbirth easier, all the money we spent for those lessons?"

The little voice interrupts again, "All those breathing lessons and you won't have to breathe even once – too bad!"

My protests stop as I see the stretcher meant for us being pushed down the hall by yawning attendants. My doctor heads for the operating room. I swallow hard and exclaim under my breath, "Ready or not, little child, here we go!"

As I am being delivered to my surgeon, I marvel at medical science; years ago, your birth might have been a difficult one for us. In some respects, we have both been given the easy way out. You will simply be lifted out of your warm nest, your small body saved from the pressures and agony of labor. I will be spared the discomfort and exhaustion caused by the long hours of labor and waiting.

I lie still on my back and watch the institutional-looking clock on the wall tick off the seconds. The doctors and nurses

Our Dear Child ✱ ✱ ✱ ✱ ✱

ready themselves for the surgery. Outside the door, and then by our side, stands your father. Within minutes, little child, you and your father and I will come face to face. What an important day this is for you – for us! As we both watch your safe delivery, our many prayers for you will have been answered. As we take you into our arms as mother, as father, our many promises to you will surround you and embrace you, and, with God's help, will begin to be fulfilled.

Love, Mom

Here At Last!

Dear Child,

Your birthday is here at last! At nine months into the pregnancy, the doctor kept assuring us, "Any time now, any day now". Two weeks after D-Day, he decided to induce labor. I shall never forget that Thursday morning. The drive to the hospital, the examination by the doctor, the X-rays showing you in breech position, the necessity for Caesarean birth.

Suddenly I was standing outside the operating room. Inside they were preparing your mother for surgery. It must have been only a few minutes, but it seemed like a brief eternity to me. The thoughts which raced through my mind? "At last, it's happening at last! What are they doing to Denise? Why haven't they come for me yet? What will she/he look like?" The nurses all smiled knowingly as they walked by. I was a dead giveaway, pacing back and forth with camera in hand: a first-time father for sure!

Then I was being ushered into the delivery room. The doctor and attendants were already at work. "It won't be long now," someone said. Denise was fully awake, a faint smile on her face. I stood by her side as our doctor reached inside her opened belly, pulled hard once or twice, then lifted you out. "It's a boy," he said. A few seconds later he whacked your backside, and your lungs burst forth in symphonic sound.

"He's just beautiful!" I exclaimed as I snapped the camera. Then you were in my arms. For nine months and two weeks, your mother had carried you. Now it was my turn. I showed you to her and she smiled. For a few precious seconds the three of us were together. Then I followed the nurses as they placed you in a "warmer" for a few minutes, then on to the nursery, where you were fingerprinted and weighed, and given your own special bed.

I was determined not to let you out of my sight, because I had a horrid fear (too many old movies, I guess) that you might get mixed up with some other baby! When you were safely nestled in the nursery, I returned to your mother. We sat and talked and held hands, then silently thanked the Lord.

After picking up your grandmother at the airport, I telephoned Denise at the hospital. She sounded confused: "The baby's with me now, but I'm not sure it's the right one!"

"What!" I exploded. Visions of horror flew through my mind. The wrong baby! "Don't do anything, I'll be right there!" Not to worry, she was simply groggy from the medicine and all the excitement. It was really you nestled close beside her in the bed, the right baby. Our little son, Christian Timothy George, here at last.

Love, Dad

Just Like Christmas Eve

Dear Child,

Welcome to the world, little Christian Timothy George! This is your day, the day your daddy and I will cherish forever. What beautiful memories you have given us on your birthday. You have made us a family – mother, father, and son.

All the waiting, the planning, the hoping and the praying we have done has come to fruition. You were well worth the long wait.

Soon the events of this day will be only memories, many of which, perhaps, will pass as you grow and bring many more moments to remember. But one thought will remain forever with me – my doctor's words only moments before your birth.

"Denise," he said, as he prepared to make the life-enabling incision, "this is just like Christmas Eve. The gift you are about to receive will keep on giving for years and years to come." I smiled at him and kept those thoughts with me to ponder long after the activities of your delivery.

Then the birth events began, experiences not only physical, but emotional and spiritual as well.

After several properly-placed incisions, my doctor lifted you from my body and exclaimed for all to hear: "It's a boy!"

A boy! Your daddy, usually a reserved and dignified gentleman, clad in cumbersome surgical greens, immediately lost all dignity, clapping his hands and jumping up and down with excitement. With the nurse's help, the doctor wrapped you in a warm blanket and placed you in your father's arms. Oh the comfort a daddy's strong, loving arms must have brought you as you entered this strange and sterile environment!

Then your daddy brought you for me to see. Tiny, red, squirmy, screaming, wrinkled skin – what a beautiful sight you were to me! My little son! In my delirious exhilaration, I could only say: "Daddy, he's got your ears!" Your daddy's comment? "He's beautiful, looks just like the Gerber baby!"

Then the staff of nurses and doctors, Daddy and you, left the operating room and headed for the nursery. The doctor finished the necessary stitching and a nurse rolled me to the recovery room.

I soon discovered that a hospital does not lend itself to recovery. Your father joined me in the recovery room; we sat together, and with incision-splitting excitement, relived the wonderful moments of our joint adventure. Then we called all our family and friends to tell them the news. Soon, a multitude of visitors came to offer us their congratulations.

Now, visiting hours are over. They have retrieved you from your hour of nursing. Your daddy and grandmother have gone. Only now, in the still and quiet of my hospital room, can I pick up my pen and try to remember in writing about our special day.

On this night, I pray, little Christian, that I can adequately record this day for you. Can mere words even begin to express the way I felt at the moment of your birth? Or the way you looked, so securely snuggled in your father's arms? Or the glow you brought to a new daddy's face? Or the tenderness I experienced when I fed you your first dinner?

I must answer, "No."

"Just like Christmas Eve," my doctor had called the moment of your birth.

Christmas Eve, indeed, for Christmas Eve expresses the giving of oneself to another, the loving and caring and sharing of one to another. And Christmas Eve anticipates the excitement of Christmas Day, and the gift God gave to his loved ones, and the loved one he gives to us this day – a gift that will keep on giving day after day, year after year.

Welcome, little Christian Timothy George.

Love, Mom

The Gift of Discernment

Dear Child,

One of the great saints of the early church was a man named Basil of Caesarea. This was a prayer he offered asking for the gift of discernment. I pass it along to you, my son, as a special gift. May you pray it often and find its answer in the wonderful grace of God that meets you and sustains you afresh every morning, all the days of your life, until finally your ship finds anchor in the "quiet harbor" of God's eternal love:

Steer the ship of my life, good Lord, to your quiet harbor, where I can be safe from the storms of sin and conflict. Show me the course I should take. Renew in me the gift of discernment, so that I can always see the right direction in which I should go. And give me the strength and the courage to choose the right course, even when the sea is rough and the waves are high, knowing that through enduring hardship and danger we shall find comfort and peace at last.

Love always, Dad

Postscript
A Parent's Prayer

Almighty God, our heavenly Parent,

You have entrusted to us a life so fragile, so vulnerable, so completely dependent.

We are afraid. How can we bear so weighty a responsibility? What if we make an uncorrectable mistake? What if we love too leniently or discipline too severely? What if….

Free us from the fear of failure. Teach us that parenthood does not come like a cake mix – in four easy steps. Only in the daily doing of it will we learn the proper balance.

Give us the grace to be good hosts. Remind us that this little one, who will walk beside us for a few short years, is only a guest in our home. We have no ironclad claims to the child's soul, body or life. Let us offer hospitality and kindness, gentle nudges and loving hands to mend the hurts.

Sustain us in the storms of life. When we have reached our limit, when the world has done its worst, help us to say, "Into thy hands, O Lord, we commit it all." In life, in death, today and every tomorrow, O thou who stillest raging winds, be near.

Through Jesus Christ, who was once a little baby, amen.

Love, Dad

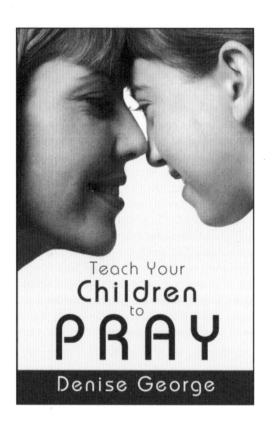

Teach Your
Children
to
PRAY

Denise George

Teach Your Children to Pray

Denise George

In a nut-shell this book is a non judgmental, practical, hands-on, I've been there approach to Christian parenting… with a wonderful, inspiring, get me started focus on prayer. Yet it doesn't compromise on the truth and the challenge of God's word. Once you start reading it you will realise the value of prayer, you will be itching to start it with your child, you will learn and your family will learn the importance of communicating with God.

Denise George, is a mother, Christian and human being. Her book is written on the back of a life time of experience, mistakes, triumphs, problems, ideas, inspiration, questions, scripture reading… and prayer.

Read this book to be challenged by the call to teach your child to pray. You'll be encouraged by the honest "I've been there," approach of the author. You're going to be inspired by the wonderful activities and ideas sections. And those really difficult questions that you've wanted to ask someone but haven't dared – have a look at the question section. There's probably someone who has asked that question before you.

Every family should read this. Every family should use this. Because every family should teach their children to pray!

'This book inspired me to pray more myself and to be creative in helping my children to pray. Denise George writes in a fresh, easy-to-read style. The book is full of suggestions to encourage your child to pray and give ideas to put legs to your children's prayers'. The author draws from her own experience as a mother of two children. Her honesty is refreshingly helpful.'

Evangelical Times

A prolific and inspirational writer Denise George is well known for writing books that are creative and biblical. Her husband Timothy is the founding dean of Beeson Divinity school.

ISBN 1-85792-941-1

aren't they Lovely
WHen they're azleep?

Lessons in unsentimental parenting

ann Benton

Aren't they lovely when they're asleep?

Lessons on unsentimental parenting

Ann Benton

Ann Benton used to run parenting skills classes in local schools. People kept saying "This is great, where do you get this stuff?" She came clean "Actually, it's from the Bible."

This book contains the wisdom distilled from Ann's popular seminars on parenting the next generation. She uses a 'God's eye view' of what we are really like in order to help people who are seeking to be responsible parents in an increasingly child-centred society.

You will learn six key concepts: *accept, beware, communicate, discipline, evaluate* and *fear the Lord*. These are applied with understanding and sensitivity.

At last – a parenting book with authority *and* easy to understand applications! Each short, punchy chapter is rounded off with thought-provoking questions that will make you want to wake them up and try some new ideas!

'A welcome and stimulating addition to contemporary literature on parenting. Ann's book helps parents to take the long view of parenting - What are we doing? We are growing adults! In taking this approach we are encouraged to look at the consequences of unhelpful practices or strategies that are all too common today.'

**Sheila M. Stephen,
counsellor and teacher on parenting skills**

'Ann Benton brings a wealth of Biblical wisdom, as well as a great deal of sound common sense to this subject. Over the past years I have learned a great deal from Ann's seminars on parenting, and also from her example as a mother. I am delighted that she has written this book, and would commend it warmly, especially to new parents.'

Sharon James, author and conference speaker

ISBN 1-85792-876-8

...of such is the kingdom

nurturing children in the light of scripture • Dr. Timothy A. Sisemore

...Of Such is the Kingdom

Nurturing Children in the Light of Scripture

Dr. Timothy A. Sisemore

Are you, and your church, bringing up children the way God wants you to?

Dr. Sisemore teaches you about - Christian parenting in a hostile world, educating children spiritually and academically, cultivating godliness, disciplining and discipling, honoring parents, how are children saved?, The church's responsibility towards its children, children's involvement in worship and sacraments.

'Anyone who has a true concern for the spiritual welfare of children in this present age must read this book!'

Mark Johnston, Pastor and Conference speaker

'Here is a straightforward, readable, challenging and practical manual - just what parents are looking for.'

Sinclair B. Ferguson,
Pastor and Adjunct Professor of Systematic Theology

Timothy Sisemore builds a practical approach to parenting and children's ministry and shows how to nurture children to be disciples. This is not a theoretical book - if you recognise the need to change your approach he shows you how to do that too.

Timothy A. Sisemore, Ph.D., earned his doctorate in clinical psychology from Fuller Theological Seminary in Pasadena, California, where he also earned the M.A. in Theology. He currently is Academic Dean and Associate Professor of Counseling at the Psychological Studies Institute in Atlanta and Chattanooga, and maintains a clinical practice at the Chattanooga Bible Institute Counseling Center.

ISBN 1-85792-514-9

Christian Focus Publications

publishes books for all ages

Our mission statement –

STAYING FAITHFUL

In dependence upon God we seek to help make His infallible Word, the Bible, relevant. Our aim is to ensure that the Lord Jesus Christ is presented as the only hope to obtain forgiveness of sin, live a useful life and look forward to heaven with Him.

REACHING OUT

Christ's last command requires us to reach out to our world with His gospel. We seek to help fulfill that by publishing books that point people towards Jesus and help them develop a Christ-like maturity. We aim to equip all levels of readers for life, work, ministry and mission.

Books in our adult range are published in three imprints.

Christian Focus contains popular works including biographies, commentaries, basic doctrine and Christian living. Our children's books are also published in this imprint.

Mentor focuses on books written at a level suitable for Bible College and seminary students, pastors, and other serious readers. The imprint includes commentaries, doctrinal studies, examination of current issues and church history.

Christian Heritage contains classic writings from the past.

Christian Focus Publications, Ltd
Geanies House, Fearn,
Ross-shire, IV20 1TW, Scotland, United Kingdom
info@christianfocus.com

For details of our titles visit us on our website
www.christianfocus.com